MAY IT PLEASE YOU, MADAM

A little book of legal whimsy

Neil Hickman

The Book Guild Ltd

First published in Great Britain in 2016 by
The Book Guild Ltd
9 Priory Business Park
Wistow Road, Kibworth
Leicestershire, LE8 0RX
Freephone: 0800 999 2982
www.bookguild.co.uk
Email: info@bookguild.co.uk
Twitter: @bookguild

Typeset in Aldine 401 BT

Printed and bound in the UK by TJ International, Padstow, Cornwall

ISBN 978 1910878 965

British Library Cataloguing in Publication Data.
A catalogue record for this book is available from the British Library.

For Sue, who needed a law book that wasn't serious

CONTENTS

FOREWORD

What is it about court proceedings that can engender so much humour? Is it the conjunction between, on the one hand, the solemnity of the occasion and the usual gravity of the subject-matter, and, on the other, the essential frivolity of most of our human thinking? Or, is it that the situation is one in which so much is SPOKEN – not just thought nor felt nor emailed nor tweeted nor watched nor just listened to – but SPOKEN, in particular by people under pressure and unaccustomed to speaking seriously to an audience for any length of time?

I am not keen on jokes by advocates. Yes, when assembled years later in a book, some of them come across as witty. But it's a form of showing off, particularly to the judge. It feels incestuous. But should a judge make jokes? There are two schools of thought. One says that it breaks the ice in a way which relaxes the litigant and makes him realise that the judge is human. The other says that it leads the litigant to think that the judge is not taking his case seriously. And the audience is captive: if it feels obliged to pretend to regard a joke from the bench as funny, does the judge abuse his position by making it? I tell myself: be pleasant but don't make jokes. At least not intentionally.

Neil Hickman must have been squirrelling away these wonderful legal anecdotes throughout his professional lifetime. Several made me laugh out loud; many collected a chuckle; still more a smile. I marked a few of the best for use in any further dreaded after-dinner speech from which no excuse might extricate me. But then I said to myself: "Most of the audience will by then have bought Neil's book and read the jokes". Ultimately, however, I countered: "But they won't have remembered them." I suspect that these stories will make no lasting impression on you at all. They are transiently delightful. Live for the moment! Buy the book! Treat yourself!

Nicholas Wilson
Justice of the UK Supreme Court
18 April 2016

PREFACE

What happens in court isn't funny, of course. We no longer hang people as a result of it; but throwing people out of their homes, ending their marriages or sending them to jail is unfunny enough in all conscience. Probably as a defence mechanism, many lawyers develop a slightly black sense of humour.

★ ★ ★

I am grateful to my colleagues in the law and on the Bench, too numerous to name individually, who have shared their experiences of funny things being said, done or written in their courts. I hope some of those things will bring a smile to your face, too. I thank Sir Stephen Sedley for allowing me to quote his incomparable *Laws of Documents* and Janet Bower, and the publishers of the *Law Society's Gazette*, for allowing me to include some of the late District Judge Jeff Bower's cartoons which originally accompanied articles in the *Gazette*. I am very grateful to Nick Goodman at the *Gazette* for locating the originals of the cartoons in the *Gazette's* records.

My thanks to Russell Hartley Jones for proof-reading page 152 – and for going the extra mile, as Court Service staff so often do, by suggesting to me what counsel might actually have said to the jury.

The splendid letter in *Arkell v Pressdram* (page 202) is reproduced by kind permission of *Private Eye* magazine.

Some names have been omitted to protect the guilty.

Neil Hickman
May Day, 2016

MAY IT PLEASE YOU, MADAM

Years ago, as a "Deputy" (that is, part-time) District Judge I used to sit at Hertford County Court, where the full-time District Judge was the redoubtable Elaine Willers. An extremely competent and thorough judge, Elaine was anxious that correct protocol should be followed in her court. As a result, she caused a notice to be displayed on the door from the waiting room into the court room, reading:

"THE DISTRICT JUDGE SHOULD BE ADDRESSED AS 'MADAM'.

It was, I suppose, inevitable that one day a nervous young advocate appearing there for the first time opened the door to the courtroom as his case was called on, saw not Elaine Willers but myself, looked back at the notice, looked once again at the three piece suit and beard, swallowed hard, and said,

"May it please you, Madam…"

And that did, in fact, happen. As did almost all the instances of, frequently unintentional, humour which follow.

GOOD MORNING, JUDGE...

F. E. Smith, who later became Lord Chancellor as Lord Birkenhead, did not suffer fools gladly, and that included fools on the Bench. On one occasion, in the days when the quality of the High Court Bench was not what it is today, a judge was rash enough to complain,

> "Mr Smith, I have been listening to you for over an hour, and I am no wiser..."

Smith instantly fired back,

> "Maybe not, my Lord. But much better informed."

It is possible, I suppose, that Smith knew his judge well and uttered the remark with a smile on his face. Once, long ago, I had to appear in the Bedford County Court before a judge not generally known for his sense of humour who had journeyed that morning all the way from Ipswich only to find that the whole of his list apart from my case had collapsed. I ventured,

"On this occasion I will not begin with 'May it please your Honour' – *because I am pretty certain that it doesn't.*"

I was rewarded with a somewhat wintry grin – and the order I sought.

★ ★ ★

Occasionally, a judge does "ask for it", and a bold advocate may be willing to oblige. Thus, back in the "good old days" a petitioner complaining of his spouse's adultery had to file a "discretion statement" setting out whether he himself had been guilty of adultery. It was open to the judge, bizarrely, to refuse to "exercise his discretion" and leave the parties married to one another (see also at page 96). And at the end of a long day of undefended divorces at Southampton, Mr Commissioner Gallop, Q.C., after reading a particularly flowery discretion statement, turned to counsel and said,

"Well, Mr Read, I don't know why these things are called discretion statements – they ought to be called indiscretion statements."

Counsel, one Terry Read, kept a straight face and responded,

"As your Lordship pleases. But it would be distinctly difficult for me to have to invite your Lordship to exercise your Lordship's *indiscretion*."

A case of a judge asking for it in a different way was Mr Justice Ridley (see page 16) asking Mr Danckwerts QC (a Chancery silk who rose to be a Lord Justice of Appeal) what authority he had for a proposition. The devastating response was:

> "Usher, fetch some elementary textbook on the
> Law of Torts."

Yes, sometimes the advocate gets very much the better of the judge.

In theory, there are three rows of seats in a courtroom. The middle row accommodates the advocates, traditionally barristers. Behind them sit the solicitors who are accompanying counsel, and their clients. And in the front row, frequently unoccupied, sit in expensive grandeur the "silks" or Queen's Counsel.

The late Niall Quinn QC, a solicitor "silk", found himself appearing before an ex-barrister judge of the dinosaur tendency. Quinn had quite properly positioned himself in the front row.

The judge, ignoring Quinn, inquired of his clerk:

> "That man in the front row – has he got a
> *certificate*?"

Having heard the judge's attempted put-down perfectly clearly, as the judge no doubt intended, Quinn languidly rose to his feet and drawled,

> "Your Honour, I have *two*. One entitles me
> to sit here [indicating the QCs' row]. *And the
> other* [Quinn also being a Recorder, or part time
> Circuit Judge] *entitles me to sit where Your Honour
> is sitting.*"

Probably just as calculated to annoy the judge as most
of the F. E. Smith-isms, though.

And it is not only judges. Back in the days when
all child care cases started off before the Magistrates,
a solicitor of my acquaintance was acting for the child
in a case where there were complicated and serious
allegations which everyone, local authority, parents, the
lot, agreed needed to be tried by a Circuit Judge. He duly
stood up before the local beaks asking for the transfer up
to the county court with which everyone agreed. The
Chairwoman of the local bench inquired indignantly,

> "Mr -------, are you suggesting that my
> colleagues and I are not intelligent enough to
> deal with this case?"

The solicitor, not in the sunniest of moods, having
been up all night attending a client at the police station,
smoothly responded,

> "Madam, I couldn't have put it more eloquently
> if I had tried."

Dealing with the inevitable appeal, the Judge
looked at him with weary resignation and said,

"We all *think* it, Mr -------. *But you bloody well had to say it out loud, didn't you?*"

before allowing the appeal. The temptation to drop advocates in it has its limits.

"CHUCK IT, SMITH"

F. E. Smith, whom we have just encountered, was the victim of a sardonic poem by G. K. Chesterton which had the refrain: "Chuck it, Smith!" But Chesterton was referring to Smith's politics rather than the sort of antics we are about to discuss.

What was probably the finest example of a judicial poker face was displayed by a county court judge, Judge Clothier QC, at Lambeth just after the war. The genial James Comyn, later a well-liked judge, was acting for a landlord seeking to evict a determined and fairly senior lady tenant on the ground that she had been a nuisance to her neighbours. She had given her evidence and the case appeared to be going her way. Comyn stood up to cross-examine.

"Madam…"

he managed to say.

At which point the tenant reached in her bag and pulled out a dead cat, which she hurled at counsel's chest. As Pussy thudded into the pin-stripes, His Honour peered over his spectacles and observed mildly,

"Madam, *if you do that again* I shall commit you for contempt."

and went on to find for the landlord.

★ ★ ★

When missiles do get thrown in the direction of the Bench, the missile of choice usually seems to be the egg, and the disgruntled litigant sometimes gets his aim right – of the three eggs thrown by a Mr Hammerton in a notable 2007 case, one actually found its target on Judge Paul Collins' suit.

Back in Victorian times, a judge similarly pelted appears to have missed the chance of minor immortality. In 1877, Vice-Chancellor Malins, sitting in the court next door to that of Vice-Chancellor Bacon, was the subject of a near-miss; and although, according to the late Sir Robert Megarry, the following exchange did take place:

Vice-Chancellor: What was that?
Mr Glasse QC: An egg.
Vice-Chancellor: Where did it come from?
Mr Glasse QC: A hen, I presume.

Malins did *not*, in fact, make the remark sometimes attributed to him concerning the egg:

"That must have been intended for my brother Bacon."

GREETING THE JUDGE

Correctly addressing a judge is a subject that keeps the writers of publications like *Debrett's* busy. With the exception of one devout Quaker two centuries ago who was permitted to decline a knighthood, every person who is appointed as a judge of the High Court is created a knight or a Dame. Yet a High Court Judge is referred to as 'Mr Justice X'.

When they got round to appointing women to the High Court Bench, it was felt that they should be called 'Mrs Justice X', irrespective of marital status, because, it was said, calling someone 'Missjustice' might be misunderstood. When, however, Alison Russell was appointed to the High Court in 2014, she put her foot down and successfully insisted that she be 'Ms Justice Russell'.

I doubt she will be the last.

Similarly, judges of the Court of Appeal are called 'Lord Justice -----', and judges of the Scottish Court of Session and Justices of the UK Supreme Court are called 'Lord', even though they are not members of the House of Lords. It's all a bit reminiscent of the wry observation attributed to Ernest Bevin when he was appointed Lord Privy Seal:

"I am neither a Lord, nor a Privy, nor a Seal."

When in 1988 Dame Elizabeth Butler-Sloss became the first woman to be appointed to the Court of Appeal, she was for some time officially known as *Lord* Justice Butler-Sloss, because that was what section 2 of the Supreme Court Act 1981 required, unless and until Parliament got round to amending it. So counsel had to use the tongue-twisting form of address: 'My Lady, Lord Justice Butler-Sloss'.

Eventually there was a modest outbreak of common sense, and in a Practice Note entitled *Mode Of Address: Dame Elizabeth Butler-Sloss* Sir Thomas Bingham, the then Master of the Rolls, describing the situation as "plainly absurd", said,

> "Nothing can for the time being be done to alter the formal position, but for informal purposes it is desirable that reference should be made to Lady Justice Butler-Sloss, so that she will be referred to in court as 'My Lady, Lady Justice Butler-Sloss'."

Similarly, the first woman to occupy the Speaker's chair in the House of Commons, Betty Harvie Anderson, insisted on being addressed as 'Mr Deputy Speaker' on the basis that the Deputy Speaker was the Deputy Speaker and the gender of the person holding the office was irrelevant. When her better known namesake Betty Boothroyd became a Deputy Speaker in 1987, however, her first act on taking the Chair was to declare firmly,

"Call me Madam!"

And, of course, you will have picked up already that, at the time of writing at any rate, you should also address a District Judge as 'Madam' – or, should the District Judge in question happen to be male, 'Sir'. But there are other possibilities.

One colleague observed,

> "In the last year I have been called 'Your Excellency' and 'Your Majesty'. Respect, man!"

To which another responded,

> "No respect in ----------. The best I've had is 'My Lord'."

And another unfeelingly observed,

> "An applicant before me on her umpteenth application for suspension of a possession warrant ran all through the range of titles before reaching 'Your Majesty'. I don't know what she said when I refused the application as I had a sudden attack of judicial deafness."

At the other extreme, when I was spelling out the terms on which I was prepared to suspend a possession order and asked the tenant whether she would comply with those terms, I was rather disarmed by the reply:

"Yes, my lovely."

A District Judge from one of the larger courts commented self-deprecatingly,

"Being called a 'fat bastard' had the merit of being half right; but which half?"

which drew the even more self-deprecating response from one of his colleagues:

"This may be a case of mistaken identity. The assumption was that *I* was sitting."

A colleague in the North was once addressed as 'cock', while down the road in Manchester:

"I have been called everything from 'your majesty' to 'me duck'. The strangest was 'your worships'. Evidently counsel believed he was also addressing the two invisible dwarfs who advise me."

Elsewhere:

"Maybe being in Essex has something to do with this, but many litigants in person see me as their 'mate' (not in the biblical sense I hasten to add)."

One District Judge politely responded to a cheery

"Thank you, mate" from a litigant by observing that he was not the litigant's mate. The reproof was cheerily accepted with,

"Oh, sorry, pal."

And a further geographical twist:

"I must sometimes give parties the impression that I am Turkish and indeed that I come from Ankara. I have often heard them remark to that effect as they leave my room... at least, I think that is what they are saying."

★ ★ ★

Note that by a curious quirk although magistrates are addressed as 'Your Worships', a Circuit Judge is merely 'Your Honour'. One County Court Judge, addressed as 'My Lord', responded,

"You Lord me too much and Honour me too little."

And another judge is supposed to have explained to a litigant,

"You may honour me, but you must not worship me."

He should be so lucky. A colleague from the circuit

bench tells of being addressed as 'ducks' by an older female litigant, and a District Judge from the same court says resignedly:

> "I've been addressed as 'love', and 'dear', as well as 'my lady' and 'your worship'. I'll take anything that isn't abusive or threatening, frankly, but then I do have low expectations!"

Another occasional (male) visitor to Hertford recalled,

> "I was once addressed as 'Madam' and, on another occasion, more accurately perhaps, as 'pompous git'."

Another District Judge who was addressed with the same adjective remarked,

> "I did once consider dealing with 'pompous old fart' as contempt, not being old at the relevant time."

You may recall that Marty Feldman rudely described the judge in the *Schoolkids' Oz* trial long ago as a 'boring old fart'.

That invaluable work of legal reference *Private Eye* commemorated this by referring to him for some while thereafter as 'Farty Meldman'. In one of the more sensible decisions he took during that trial, the judge, the late Michael Argyle QC, declined to rise to the bait. While that is generally thought to be the most prudent reaction for the judge to adopt, readers are advised not to conduct their own experiments.

Thus one Gray, editor of the *Birmingham Daily Argus*, in 1900 took exception to Mr Justice Darling "advising" the local press as to how it should report the evidence in an obscenity case he was conducting:

> "If anyone can imagine Little Tich upholding his dignity upon a point of honour in a public-house, he has a very fair conception of what Mr. Justice Darling looked like in warning the Press against the printing of indecent evidence. His diminutive Lordship positively glowed with judicial self-consciousness... No newspaper can exist except upon its merits, a condition from which the Bench, happily for Mr. Justice Darling, is exempt. There is not a journalist in Birmingham who has anything to learn from the impudent little man in horse-hair, a microcosm of conceit and empty-headedness... One is almost sorry that the Lord Chancellor had not another relative to provide for on the day that he selected a new judge from among the larrikins of the law. One of Mr. Justice Darling's biographers states that 'an eccentric relative left him much money'. That misguided testator spoiled a successful bus conductor."

Although the ancient offence of 'scandalising a judge' has since fallen into disuse, it proved expensive for Mr

Gray. £100 fine (equivalent to over £10,000 now) and £25 costs in the Divisional Court.

And while Mr Stephen Balogh, son of the distinguished economist Lord Balogh, did not actually receive a separate penalty for informing the formidable Mr Justice Melford Stevenson:

> "You are a humourless automaton, why don't you self destruct?"

that was only because Melford had already hit him with a six–month jail sentence for attempting to enliven a tedious trial at St. Alban's Crown Court by releasing the contents of a cylinder of laughing gas into the air conditioning system.

Freeing him from jail, the Court of Appeal concluded that because he had been caught before putting the plan into effect, he was not actually guilty of contempt. In a characteristically enigmatic comment, Lord Denning suggested that:

> "Insults are best treated with disdain – save where they are gross and scandalous."

How you categorise "humourless automaton" is, I suppose, a matter of opinion.

It would certainly be inadvisable to emulate the forthright female defendant appearing before Mr Justice Ridley, probably not one of the more inspired appointments to the High Court Bench (see page 4). Annoyed by Ridley's conduct of the trial, she informed him,

"You are nothing but a little bit of sheep's turd."

Unwisely, instead of ignoring her, Ridley responded,

"No, I am not!"

Predictably, on her way down to the cells the defendant kept shouting,

"Sheep's turd! Sheep's turd!"

Ridley might have tried the approach of one judge when a defendant who was being led away from the court after being remanded in custody, shouted,

"You're just a fucking stupid bastard."

Completely unfazed, the judge had him brought back into the dock.

"If you wish to speak with your solicitor, kindly wait until you have left my courtroom."

A more direct approach was once adopted by a Crown Court judge, now deceased, who had just sentenced a man to seven years' imprisonment. As the man turned toward the door at the back of the dock he called out,

"You're a stupid fucking c★★t!"

The judge invited the defendant to return to the dock and said,

> "Sit down, Mr -------. And listen to me carefully.
>
> You and I will shortly be leaving this building. I will be going in my comfortable car to my comfortable home where I will spend the evening with my family, have what I want to eat, and do what I choose. You will be leaving in a filthy van for an even filthier prison where you will spend the next three and a half years banged up with two other incompetent criminals who got caught. On the way you may care to ask yourself which of us is a stupid fucking c★★t.
>
> Now take him down."

Nowadays, even if you avoid annoying a newspaper man, Facebook awaits, and a litigant appearing before one judge posted a message on Facebook to the effect that Judge D---- was "a c★★t and a w★★★★r".

He was hauled up before another judge in the court, fortunately in the days before it was mandatory for such judgments to go on a public website.

The disgruntled litigant admitted the offence and accepted that he'd gone too far. Silkily, the judge explained the position:

> "Now, if you go back to the pub in the village where you live, and you take yourself into the darkest and most remote corner of the bar, and

you gaze into your pint glass, and you murmur quietly into your beer that Judge D----- is a c★★t and a w★★★★r, that is perfectly acceptable and indeed understandable.

But it is not acceptable to be putting this on Facebook. Do you understand?"

He then gave him 28 days' suspended anyway. Honour was probably satisfied.

★ ★ ★

On a slightly different tack, certain judges acquire nicknames. I do not need to explain how Henry Hawkins, Lord Brampton (1817-1907), came by the soubriquet of "'Anging 'Enry 'Awkins", but the explanation would also deal with Mr Justice Avory (1851-1935) a.k.a. "The Acid Drop" or "'Anging 'Orace". Similarly, the nicknames of Crown Court judges – "Basher" and "The Smiling Assassin" – speak for themselves. But one judge acquired a nickname which, while appearing derogatory, was in fact the product of admiration from colleagues.

The District Judge in question was dealing with a warring couple arguing over the meagre spoils of their doomed marriage. Eventually, it got down to two identically desirable sofas, one black, the other white. Who should have which one? As the husband expatiated on the fact that because his ex-wife had expressed a particular preference for the black one it should, in fact, go to him, as giving her what she *wanted* wouldn't be *fair*, the judge pulled out a ten-pence coin, turned to the husband and demanded, "Heads or tails?"

This robust approach to not allowing the court to be cluttered up with nonsense earned the judge concerned the proud title of "Tosser".

★ ★ ★

Addressing the judge is one thing; but how do you address the court itself? One Italian lawyer had no doubt. He sent an email addressed to 'The Illustrious Romford County Court', which might have surprised the judge, now retired, who once suggested to me that only a very foolhardy judge would walk from the station to the court at Romford, rather than taking a taxi.

Addressing letters to the judge has its hazards. One litigant tried desperately hard to impress the two District Judges who had been dealing with his case with an envelope magnificently addressed to:

> The Honourable Mrs Justice A--- QC,
> BA(Cantab), BCL(Oxon);
> The Honourable Mrs Justice B--- QC,
> BA(Oxon), LLM(Cantab).

which heroically achieved ten errors in four lines, but merely drew the deadpan observation from District Judge A--- (an Oxford history graduate):

> "Why are they suggesting I went to Cambridge?"

Probably furthest north on the obsequiousness front, though one sympathises, a defence to a claim for possession of a rented property implored the judge for mercy and concluded:

> "May God guide you as you rule. Thank you, Your Majesty."

A slight variation on the theme, the court form for making an application to set a judgment aside invites the applicant to say: "What level of Judge does your hearing need?" That possibly deserved the response it received from one London litigant:

> "A SENSIBLE ONE."

And the form for giving notice of appeal invites the appellant to answer the question, "What order do you seek?". Manchester trumped London on this occasion with the reply:

> "That District Judge X be sacked."

Sorry, but he/she wasn't.

LAWYERS SPEAK IN CODE

Once the lawyer has managed to say good morning to the judge, the language you will hear bears a passing resemblance to English, but sometimes all is not what it seems.

You probably know that advocates refer to one another as 'my learned friend'.

There is good sense in that. Treat your opponent with courtesy, even when he appears to be talking absolute nonsense. It may turn out that he isn't talking nonsense at all. And it is, after all, the argument you are dealing with, not the individual putting the argument forward.

When I started in the law, however, there was an attitude among certain members of the Bar that solicitors were a distinctly inferior breed. It was not until 2008 that solicitor advocates appearing in the Crown Court were permitted to wear wigs like ~~proper advocates~~ barristers.

And that mind-set meant that while counsel (a barrister) on the other side should be referred to as 'my learned friend', a solicitor advocate should be 'my friend'.

Some solicitor advocates (including myself)

occasionally took a perverse delight in insisting on the "correct" form of address. I remember once I was appearing for the defendant in the county court. I do not recall whether counsel for the plaintiff had managed to get thoroughly up my nose in the robing room, or whether I was following the old, but quite sound, advice:

> "If the law is against you, concentrate on the merits of your case. If you have no merits, concentrate on the law. And if you have neither law nor merits, *give the opposing advocate hell!*"

At all events, counsel introduced the case to the judge:

> "Your Honour, I appear for the plaintiff in this case; my learned friend Mr Hickman appears for the defendant."

I leaned over and murmured, loudly enough for him to hear but sufficiently quietly that the judge missed it,

> "I'm not learned, you know."

It threw him completely. I can only hope, in mitigation, that the defendant *deserved* to win.

Giving the opposing advocate hell can be taken to extremes. I am assured that on one occasion an inexperienced but distinctly pompous advocate was instructed to deal with care proceedings, a field with which he was not familiar. Having made the mistake of irritating all the other advocates in the case in the robing room, he asked them what the Wechsler test was (it is, essentially, a form of IQ test). He was told with a straight face by the other advocates that it involved a wooden box which was plugged into the mains, the subject being asked to place his hand on top of the box...

Came the hearing, the author of a psychological report was being cross examined:

"Now, Doctor, this Wechsler test. It involves a wooden box that you plug into the wall, does it not?"

Witness, almost at a loss for words, to judge: "Your Honour, do I have to answer that?"

Judge (a wise old bird who knew exactly what had been going on without needing to be told), looking directly and severely at the mischief makers on the advocates' bench: *"No, Doctor, you do not."*

★ ★ ★

You will hear advocates say, "With respect...".

Be aware that this does not quite mean what it appears to mean. The suggested translation from Lawyerese into English –

'With respect' = 'You are wrong';
'With great respect' = 'You are quite wrong';

'With the utmost respect' = 'Send for the men in white coats!'

– is not entirely wide of the mark.

One Usher I encountered in the Magistrates' Court was fully alive to this. The Magistrates had retired to consider their verdict, taking their clerk with them. (I will just say at this point that this particular clerk was a gentleman with whom I did not always see eye to eye, and the feeling was entirely mutual.)

"You two hate one another, don't you?" she observed.

"Whatever gives you that idea?" I said.

"You were being so polite to one another!"

★ ★ ★

A more common problem is when the advocate is required to advance a case with which he disagrees. I do not mean that on the facts he thinks the client's case should fail – every advocate with half a brain knows that an account which looks utterly implausible may turn out to be true, and that one which appears overwhelmingly convincing may prove to be nonsense. As Mr Justice Megarry put it in a 1970 case:

"As everybody who has anything to do with the law well knows, the path of the law is strewn with examples of open and shut cases which, somehow, were not; of unanswerable charges which, in the event, were answered; of inexplicable conduct, which was fully explained…"

Or, as Lord Justice Sedley observed in a furious dissenting judgment in 2008:

"There can be few practising lawyers who have not had the experience of resuming their seat in a state of hubristic satisfaction, having called a respectable witness to give apparently cast-iron evidence, only to see it reduced to wreckage by ten minutes of well-informed cross-examination or convincingly explained away by the other side's testimony. Some have appeared in cases in which everybody was sure of the defendant's guilt, only for fresh evidence to emerge which makes it clear that they were wrong. As Mark Twain said, the difference between reality and fiction is that fiction has to be credible. In a system which recruits its judges from practitioners, judges need to carry this kind of sobering experience to the bench. It reminds them that you cannot be sure of anything until all the evidence has been heard, and that even then you may be wrong."

What if the advocate is instructed to put forward a case which he knows, or believes, is bad in law?

You will read in some books that counsel's duty is

to draw the court's attention to relevant authorities even when they harm his client's case. Another approach was demonstrated by a young advocate who charmingly suggested to me that I should dismiss an application made by a litigant in person. After I had duly found in her opponent's favour, she politely held the door open for him to leave, half closed the door after him, observed,

> "You will have noted, Sir, that I said: '*I am instructed* to submit that…'. That is because I know as well as you do that the submission is pants."

beamed at me, and left.

That young woman, I thought, will go far. Sadly, it was away from my court.

… and so I have to ask myself – does the withdrawal of the defendant's admission in any way prejudice the load of tripe that is put forward as the claimant's case?

There are other approaches. Thus, what one judge described as the accurate opening submissions of counsel:

> "The Court's task is an unenviable one: in terms of the evidence adduced by and on behalf of the adult Respondents it is submitted that the search for the truth will be the forensic equivalent of looking for a needle in a row of haystacks. Diogenes travelled the ancient world looking for an honest man; he looked in vain; the Court's horizons are somewhat more restricted but the search will be as unrewarding. Rarely can a Court have been treated to such a parade of witnesses for whom truth, candour and insight were demonstrably such alien concepts."

"I was amused and impressed," remarked His Honour. Mr Justice Briggs in another case plainly wasn't:

> "Rather than admit the inevitable, Mr H--- wriggled and evaded with imagination but without candour, and this became the hallmark of his evidence in cross examination, all the more so in relation to more directly relevant events. In the result, I did not find Mr H---'s evidence to be of any assistance to the court, save in the sense that he demonstrated the truth of that which the Club sought to prove as to the

lack of integrity with which he participated in relevant events."

Or, faced with someone who one can say with hindsight ought never to have become a company director, and certainly not alongside her spectacularly dishonest brother:

> "I found M----- to be a most unsatisfactory witness. She appeared to have come to court determined to make good a few factual propositions, if necessary by constant repetition, and to do so regardless whether a particular question called for that response. Despite a ready tendency to avoid answering questions based on documents by asserting (usually truthfully) that she had not seen the document before, and a frequent recourse to an absence of recollection, such evidence as she did give on matters of any detail was constantly at variance with the contemporary documents, and all too often with her own previous testimony... Some of it appeared to have been invented on the spot, to extricate her from obvious difficulties."

He would perhaps have been assisted by the old fashioned usher at one of the London county courts who approached a witness whose potential truthfulness aroused his suspicions.

Usher: Do you wish to take the oath on the Bible, or to affirm?

Witness: I'll swear on the Bible, please.

Usher (looking intently at witness): *Are you sure…?*

To similar effect are the old sayings: 'Truth will out, even in an affidavit' and 'As unreliable as an eye-witness.'

IN CHANCERY

Even the majority of lawyers tend to look slightly askance at the Chancery Division and what goes on there.

You might suppose that 'Chancery' has something to do with 'chance' and that, accordingly, if you are in Chancery you might as well flip a coin.

Wrestling has adopted the term for a variety of head-lock. Apparently, 'head chancery' is a shortened way of saying 'head in chancery', 'in chancery' meaning in a hopeless situation.

But the word is a contraction of 'Chancellery' and acknowledges the fact that the Courts of Chancery grew up in the days when the Lord Chancellor not only knew something about the law, but was actually the chief judge. Some of the rules of the common law operated in an arbitrary and unjust way – or that was how it appeared – and the Lord Chancellor took it into his hands to make things work more fairly.

The problem with that, of course, is that one person's idea of what is fair may not be another's. And by the seventeenth century, it was being said of 'equity', the law as administered in the Court of Chancery, that

"Equity is a roguish thing: for law we have a measure, know what to trust to; equity is according to the conscience of him that is Chancellor, and as that is larger or narrower, so is equity. 'Tis all one as if they should make the standard for the measure we call a foot, a Chancellor's foot; what an uncertain measure would this be? One Chancellor has a long foot, another a short foot, a third an indifferent foot: 'tis the same thing in a Chancellor's conscience."

Or, as is sometimes said,

"Equity varies with the length of the Chancellor's foot."

That led a number of Lord Chancellors to try to codify the way in which equity should work. There developed a number of rather vacuous but high-sounding expressions known as the Maxims of Equity. One of the best known is that

"He who comes to Equity must come with clean hands."

which led to a tale which Lord Denning used to tell about one of his colleagues, Lord Justice Donald Somervell. Somervell was a former MP who had been rather more successful than Ridley in making the transition from making the law to applying it. He was, as Denning observed, "a good Common Lawyer", but had been put in the Chancery side of the Court of Appeal, and made great play of washing his hands very thoroughly before going into court.

One day, however, Somervell arrived late, and explained why. He had had a puncture and had to change the wheel.

> "There he was with his hands all dirty. We said: 'Aren't you going to wash your hands before you go into Court?' He said: 'I don't need to. We're in the Divorce Court today'."

Over the years, of course, one Lord Chancellor after another tried to avoid the reproach of equity varying with the length of his foot, and Chancery lawyers earned a reputation for a particular kind of dour, over-literal approach to language.

Common lawyers mischievously tell of the Chancery barrister stuck helplessly at the bottom of an escalator, unable to proceed.

> There was a sign reading DOGS MUST BE CARRIED. And he didn't have a dog.

And one judge in one of the bigger court centres claims to have circulated among his colleagues a memorandum commenting deadpan on the fact that the word *gullible* isn't in the Oxford English Dictionary.

Two days later he received a grumpy note telling him that

he was completely wrong, that it appeared on page xxx, that the definition was such-and-such, and that the etymology was… etc.

Signed by Mr Justice ------ of – where else? – the Chancery Division of the High Court.

HELLO, MRS MALAPROP

Some people have a remarkable ability to mix words up; the examples actually uttered by Mrs Malaprop in Sheridan's play *The Rivals* seem uninspired by comparison.

One court clerk demonstrated a promising talent when she disappeared into the court store room, emerged having cut her hand on something and bleeding profusely, and, thinking of *haemophilia*, cheerily announced:

"I must be an 'ermaphrodite!"

She kept up the good work with the explanation for wearing a fake tan in the depths of winter –

"If I don't, I look like an Albanian."

– before excelling herself on receiving news of the departure of one of the court's judges to Clerkenwell County Court, whose premises are in *Gee Street*:

"Oh, I thought you said Judge ---- was *wearing a G-string…*"

She was in good company.

When someone doesn't do as they are told, a judge will sometimes endorse on an order what is called a 'penal notice', informing the offending party that he risks being punished for contempt. It's not an everyday term, so one can sympathise with the indignant wife who wrote in complaining about her husband's solicitors who

> "...refused to give me my husband's financial statement and they put severe pressure on me in court and tried to gain a *penile notice* against me for not exchanging statements and they are now refusing to give me Mr ------'s statement. Is there any chance I can request a *penile notice* to put against Mr ------- and/or his solicitor for not complying...?"

Sadly, the law could not fulfil her request literally, but she conjured up a splendidly memorable image.

Another irate ex-spouse may have been nearer the mark[1] than she knew when, complaining how her ex-partner's approach to contact with their son was interfering with the son's sporting activities:

> "...and he has a rugby *torment* on my weekend."

One eminent London District Judge recalled that his mother attended his swearing-in, pointed to the Bench, and asked

---

1   Says someone who, being bad at sport, spent seven fairly miserable years at a Rugby playing public school.

"Is that where you *persecute* people?"

A tenant, defending a claim for possession by his landlord by reference to disrepair at the property referred repeatedly, both in his Counterclaim and in his oral evidence, to his claim against his Landlord for "*despair*".

The mordant comment from another District Judge was:

"Is that the same as *distress for rent*?"

(Sorry, lawyerese).

An applicant seeking a non-molestation injunction asserted that:

"I went abroad to look after my father who had *ammonia*…"

Another matrimonial case produced a statement which might have referred to depression, or could, I suppose, have been literally true:

"My wife is suffering from *depreciation*."

One litigant was concerned by a rude letter from the other party. His complaint?

"*Defecation* of character!"

Though he could have fared worse; he could have

shared the fate of the litigant, who was *not* suing Her Majesty's Revenue and Customs, who complained of being

"…fiscally assaulted by the Defendant."

SPEAKING THE SAME LANGUAGE

Sometimes a witness gives a surprising answer to a question. Quite often, advocates forget to talk in language that the witness will understand. But I have some sympathy for the barrister cross-examining Joseph Hunt, an accessory to the Radlett murder in 1823. One thing that particularly appalled people about the murderer Thurtell and his accomplices was the fact that immediately after a particularly brutal murder they calmly sat down together to a supper of pork chops.

Hunt was questioned about the supper:

"Was the supper *postponed*?"

"No, it was *pork*."

Somewhat more prosaic was the case in which a male fork lift truck driver had collided with a fork lift truck driven by the female Claimant. The Defendant employer defended on the basis that the two had been in a relationship and fallen out, and the male had deliberately rammed the Claimant out of spite, so it was not in the course of his employment. Counsel for the employer asked the Claimant, "You had been in a relationship with Mr XXX?'" Much to counsel's surprise, she vehemently denied it. He tried two or three more forms of question with the same result, the Claimant becoming more and more obviously offended at the suggestion. Sounding slightly desperate, counsel asked, "But you have admitted having sexual relations with him?" The Claimant laughed with obvious relief at receiving a question she could understand and said

> "Oh yes - we've had quite a few one-night stands... but I never had a *relationship* with him!"

"Strange what offends people in Doncaster," remarked the District Judge before whom that one unfolded.

As in Doncaster, so in Birmingham, it would appear. I was told that on one occasion in that admirable city the perfectly reasonable question put by counsel in cross-examination:

> "Are you and Mr -------- in a relationship, Miss So and So?"

prompted the remarkable intervention from the Judge:

> "Miss ------, you and I are in a *relationship*, the *relationship* of judge and advocate."

Some would call that missing the point.

★ ★ ★

The problem exists with jurors as well as witnesses. Thus one presiding judge proposed to his colleagues that they should give the following direction to the jury, after the usual homily about not speaking to others:

> "An important principle of our jury system is that what happens in the jury room is private and we do not wish to hear of it. However, very rarely something may happen in your room which causes one or more of you real concern. If that very rare situation were to arise, please bring it to my attention as soon as possible."

One of the other judges in the court concerned revealed what happened next:

> "Today when the jury returned with their verdict they sent the following note signed by all 12 – 'Your Honour, as the jury we found it very distracting and stomach turning that your prosecuting Barrister was continuously picking his nose, ears, etc. rubbing between fingers and then eating it. Is that what your lordship had in mind?'"

Needless to say, observed the judge concerned, the defendant was acquitted within 20 minutes.

Another version of being at cross purposes arose as soon as the defendant arrived at court. At many court centres, the county court and the magistrates' court are in the same building. And the usher at Dudley County

Court was approached by a man who, in a broad Black Country accent, announced:

> "Yam 'ere for a possession 'earing and oi can't foind moy name on the list."

The usher enquired whether it was a mortgage possession hearing or a rent possession hearing.

> "Naow," came the reply. "Cannabis!"

WHAT DID YOU SAY
YOUR NAME WAS?

Bedford Hospital used to be graced by a charming urologist who rejoiced in the name of Waterfall, and was no doubt familiar with the seminal peer-reviewed paper on urinary incontinence authored by – who else? – Messrs Splatt and Weedon.

I believe Sheffield boasted a spinal surgeon named Jellinek.

And the courts regularly see litigants and others with singularly apt names. One colleague had a case with two housing officers from a Housing Association called Miss Perfect and Miss Locksmith. What a team!

Or a fast-track road traffic case where counsel for the claimant was Mr Perfect, counsel for the Defendant Mr Treasure.

Where did the accident occur? On one occasion it actually was at Morton's Fork (in a residential district of Milton Keynes).

One District Judge, making an order on paper which she appreciated the defendant might not be too happy about, noticed with mild concern that their name was Voodoo Dolls.

Another tried a small claim: "Freedom Days v Littledean Jail", while another tried one called "Nosal v Blower", and yet another heard "UPS Ltd v Downes".

One was delighted to encounter a road traffic case where the allegations were that the defendant drove too fast, failed to brake and failed to avoid the accident. The defendant's name? Mr Brakewell.

Best not to think too hard, perhaps, about the parties to the case of "Bobbett v Stiff".

(You remember the fate of Wayne Bobbett?)
And in similar vein, perhaps the exclusively female firm of plumbers who appeared in one small claim had allowed themselves a little smile as they chose the business name "Stopcocks".

But it was surely most appropriate that a statement in open court had to be made in libel proceedings after a magazine publisher accepted that it had wrongly alleged that the claimant was a convicted drug smuggler. The person who had actually served time for smuggling cocaine was the previous owner of the yacht which the Claimant now owned. The Claimant's name? Nicholas Tristram *Cokes*.

★ ★ ★

According to *Punch* long ago, summoned before the Feltham magistrates for exceeding the speed limit was "a man named Snail."

Punch's comment was, "…no official joke was made. Incidentally, why is it that Mr Justice Darling never gets a real chance like this?"

You may feel that the Chairman of the Bench whom we meet at page 89 made up for it. As for the late Mr Justice Darling, who was distinctly fond of attempting to be funny, few if any of his jests survive transfer to the printed page. The splendid invective of the Editor of the *Birmingham Daily Argus* concerning His Lordship, fares better, however, as we saw at page 15.

Mr Justice Darling would have had a field day with the defendant in one possession claim encountered by a Deputy District Judge. He had run up arrears of £1,700. He had not made contact with his landlord, ignored both the notice of the proceedings and the proceedings themselves, did not file a defence and did not attend the hearing. His name? Mr Denial.

Occasionally the occupations of parties appear too apt for words as well. There used to be a procedure called an affiliation summons, by which the mother of a child born out of wedlock could apply to the magistrates, seeking maintenance from the child's father. One father in such a case was duly sworn and asked his occupation.

"Horizontal borer" came the reply, with a completely straight face which the Magistrates struggled to match.

DID THAT REALLY HAPPEN?

The small claims list in the county court throws up some surprises.

You may have read that Margaret Thatcher had, shall we say, a dramatic effect on the coal mining industry. There was a distinct air of wonderment on the part of the District Judge who, a couple of days after the death of the Iron Lady was announced, found himself looking at the papers in a small claim, and learned that, contrary to what he had supposed, she had not killed off mining in North East Derbyshire…

> "I am looking at a case summary for a small claim re breach of local Rules of Allotments.
>
> The Defendants are tenants of ten allotment plots at XXX. In breach of… etc… the Defendants have sunk a well, and dug a small open cast coal mine on the allotments."

I am assured the following actually happened:

> "Defendant, beset by financial and other worries, cannot stand it any more and throws

himself out of fifth floor window of his flat. His fall is broken – and he survives – when he lands on a swing seat with a padded roof cover. The swing seat is demolished and to add to his woes he has now been sued by the owner of the swing seat who in addition is claiming the cost of cleaning the bloodstained throw she wrapped around him to stem the copious bleeding."

As the District Judge in whose small claims list this claim appeared laconically observed:

"I heard the claim on the ground floor, just in case."

What does one say about

"…the claim for damages relating to the Claimants' complaint that they got inadequate entertainment on holiday because they did not like the music? They complained the music played in the hotel bar by the band was Spanish music."

They had gone on holiday to Spain. The District Judge said "Claim dismissed", for a start. Or how about

"…the claimant who sued his holiday company because the toilets in the Taj Mahal were not air conditioned, contrary to the promise of 100% air conditioned luxury touring in India?"

Moving on from Delhi belly, one small claims list concerned a malfunctioning colonic irrigation machine.

The Defendant's aggrieved pre-action letter to the Claimant said (in capitals, naturally):

> "I AM VERY SURPRISED TO RECEIVE A LETTER REGARDING CONCERNS AS WE HAVE HAD A NUMBER OF PHONE CONVERSATIONS AND NO-ONE HAS EVER MENTIONED ANY ISSUES."

The District Judge offered this case observed:

> "I feel that, after almost 40 years in the law, I have finally reached the bottom."

Several colleagues rose to the implied challenge to find even worse puns, with

> "I am sure you will flush out the issues in the course of the hearing!"

> "Were bog standard directions given?"

> "Was the hearing listed for the convenience of the parties, in public?"

and

> "The Claim will be dealt with in the early morning motions list."

Serious 'inconvenience' was experienced by the claimant in another case, which speaks for itself:

> "The claimant walked down the stairs with intention of using the toilet. There a sign on the door of the men's toilet indicating that the ladies' toilet was to be used, and the claimant knew that work was taking place inside the men's toilet. A bucket containing tools was present in the passageway. The Claimant walked past the bucket, pushed open the door of the ladies' toilet, stepped inside, and immediately fell into an open manhole."

Another small claim concerned an unpaid vet's bill for carrying out a post mortem on a tortoise.

A colleague enquired:

> "Did the defendant have to shell out in the end?"

and, after some comments which I shall spare you because they related rather more to the substance of the claim than to the search for dreadful puns, the same writer concluded:

> "…the discussion has taught us something."

★ ★ ★

The wording of the defence in a fairly substantial personal injury claim made the judge concerned raise an eyebrow or two:

"It is denied that on the said date the claimant was carrying out his duties as alleged or that the accident occurred in the manner described. The claimant had placed a full bag of plastic recyclables onto a sorting tray at the top of the ramp, and then proceeded to climb on top of it and simulate sexual intercourse with the said bag. *For the avoidance of doubt, such action did not form part of the claimant's duties.* The claimant then slipped off the bag and fell onto the ramp on his front."

And the way the defence is conducted may be remarkable, as well. Thus:

"The claimant (a man in his seventies) sued a bus company for injuries he suffered when he was trapped in the bus door while exiting. The bus company counterclaimed for their damaged bodywork caused by his frantic attempts to alert the driver as he was dragged down the road. As a final twist of the knife, the bus company refused to consent to adjourn the trial despite the claimant's wife's sudden death the night before."

"Record damages for claimant," suggested my informant, and I doubt he was far wrong.

★ ★ ★

Sometimes it's not just the parties who stretch the

imagination. The Metropolitan Police succeeded in astonishing one very experienced colleague by turning up at court to arrest one of the parties appearing before him. Why the astonishment? Let him explain…

"The police turned up at court yesterday, called by a wife who complained that her husband had breached an injunction by being within so many metres of her. How? Because he was sitting in the same court room on an application in the dispute! I kid you not."

Improbable things happen before immigration judges, as well. One can share the surprise of the judge who wrote of:

"… my bail applicant yesterday who was not deported on Monday because when he got to the Airport he had three bags and no one would pay the excess baggage charge!"

But that was nothing to the astonishment of the immigration judge who recounted to me the story of an Iranian whom we shall call Mr Z:

"Mr Z is an Iranian. He was married to a lass of Christian descent who for reasons unknown had decided to have something insulting about Jesus tattooed in a confidential place about her person. As a gesture of solidarity he decided to have something insulting about the Prophet

Mohammad tattooed on his person (in the sense in which they used the word in 1824 – see page 110). All was well until wife was sadly killed in an accident and Mr Z married a second lady who turned out to be a devout Muslim. When she saw him in all his glory she screamed and reported him to the religious police. He apparently convinced the relevant tribunal that if he were removed to Iran he would be remarkably fortunate if it were only the relevant part of him that was cut off."

"Tattooists are going to be in demand when the news of this decision gets out," remarked my informant.

At the other end of the scale, in the dry surroundings of the Chancery Division, Mr Justice Henderson struck down the will of Bane (pronounced "Barnay", apparently) Kostic, who

"...made a will leaving an estate of £8.2m to the Conservative Party. It was common ground that he suffered from delusions that 'dark forces' were conducting a 'sinister and highly organised international conspiracy' against him in which family members were implicated, and that his delusions included the belief that the Conservative Party through the agency of Margaret Thatcher could save the country from such dark forces..."

Although Mr Kostic did not succeed in handing £8.2m

to the Conservative Party, he did succeed in handing £900,000-odd to the various lawyers involved. Dickens' portrayal of the Court of Chancery swallowing up the entire estate in *Jarndyce v Jarndyce* remains relevant.

And in the humbler surroundings of the magistrates' court, a very good instance of the incredible turning out to be true was of one defendant accused of fare dodging. He insisted that it had not been him on the bus and that some unknown and malicious third party had given his details to the ticket inspector.

"And," he insisted, "I have got a really good alibi."

All right, thought the bench with considerable scepticism. Tell us.

"At the time when I was supposedly on the bus 10 miles away, I was in this courtroom being fined."

A check of the court records showed that this was indeed the case.

★ ★ ★

Back in the days when we had tax discs on cars, I acted for a client who was charged with fraudulent evasion of excise duty. Client had sent off for the tax disc for his newly restored car (he said) but it hadn't appeared from Swansea for absolutely ages and so, like a clot, he displayed in his car the label from a Guinness bottle. On the inevitable prosecution for fraudulently displaying this non-tax disc, the question arose: Had he actually acted fraudulently? As the law then stood, it mattered that he said he had actually paid the tax and that it was all down to Swansea's inefficiency. The Bench looked sceptical as the client gave his evidence.

"What arrived in the post on Monday of this week, Mr ----?"

"A tax disc." (which he produced)

"And what arrived in the post on Tuesday morning?" [See at this point: "Never ask a question to which you don't know the answer" – p. 130]

"A tax disc." (which, again, he produced)

The Chairman on the Bench smiled, probably sensing where this was going.

"And what arrived in the post on *Wednesday* morning?"

The production of the third tax disc prompted sniggering from the Bench and a rueful expression from the prosecutor, and persuaded the magistrates that the Defendant's tale that DVLA was a shambles had some substance to it. He was acquitted, but with the advice that he would do well not to be such a blithering idiot in future.

* * *

The litigant who expected the Child Support Agency to behave competently

You can understand why mediation is the flavour of the month in many situations. How would any trial judge have arrived at a sensible solution to the following:

"A one-man-band cleaner sued local solicitors (small firm) for failure to make payment in lieu of notice when cancelling their cleaning contract with him. Solicitors regularly advertise through local radio station.

Defence shows that the Claimant telephoned local radio presenters during their live breakfast show and enquired whether they knew of the solicitors – yes, came the answer, they advertise with us.

Response – 'Well, I'm the poor sod who has to clean their offices. Tell them they've run out of washing up liquid at their --------- office.'

Indignant defence says Claimant could have notified re lack of washing up liquid in a more reasonable manner, damage to professional reputation locally, breakdown of trust, complete loss of sense of humour situation leading to termination of contract for breach, etc".

The case settled on the basis of an apology for the broadcast remarks, and payment of the cleaner's issue fee, with the claim being dismissed.

"Shame!" commented the District Judge. "I would have enjoyed trying that one!"

[Mordant comment from another District Judge:

"Admit it, you just wanted to be able to say 'You've been taken to the cleaners!'".]

One debtor succeeded in making history in a small way back in 2011, as a result of bragging on Facebook about how she had been successfully avoiding being served with court papers. This was drawn to the attention of the local District Judge who made an order that the debtor in question could be validly served with the papers in question *by being informed of them via Facebook.*

So you definitely think it's too late to reject?

DID THEY REALLY SAY THAT?

One District Judge hearing a contact dispute was informed in a witness statement that

> "…the Court will note from the medical notes obtained from the ------- Hospital that this was not the first time the Respondent had taken his own life."

As he wryly observed: 'Ain't the NHS wonderful these days?'

The wonders of the NHS were not sufficient to account for what happened when a customer rang up Abbey National and explained, as told to me by a member of the court staff who had been working at the Abbey at the time, that she would be unable to make payments on her loan because she was having a hysterectomy. A little while later the same customer rang up and said that she would be unable to make payments on her loan because she had had a miscarriage.

"I think," remarked my colleague thoughtfully, "that you need to be a good liar to remember the last lie you told." Quite so.

You should sometimes remember to look at a calendar, too. As one District Judge resignedly reported:

> "Today a defendant in a mortgage possession action blamed her financial woes on the destruction of the Twin Towers."

She had overlooked the fact that this had occurred some two years before she had purchased the property in question.

★ ★ ★

What does one make of the litigant who wrote:

> "I have been forced to commit suicide and I refuse to do so…"

As the claim form in which this remarkable assertion appeared continued:

> "[I] request to the court to suit me with a male sexual partner in a blessed marriage that will last forever. He has to be handsome, tall, rich, educated, clean, have a sense of humour to live with me and my family in my home… I want my weekly wages as world peace advocator."

I am afraid the District Judge who encountered it unkindly struck it out.

Ho! Ho! Yonder knave thought that I would adjourn his case simply because he has big black spots all over him!

Another litigant wrote to the court asking for an adjournment:

> "Unfortunately I suffered a fatal accident on Monday and my doctor says I will be unable to travel to attend Court for two weeks."

and one is relieved, to some extent, by the respondent who wrote:

"During our relationship there were many incidents where I was physically attacked. None, I have to say, that were fatal…"

The NHS may be wonderful. Some local authorities are less so. Thus an indignant letter received by a judge from a grandmother embroiled in care proceedings:

"…and one of the local authority letters said I was dead. This was news to me…"

A different form of "Did they really say that?" was exemplified by the motorist who was stopped on the M6 Toll in Staffordshire because he was driving at 94 mph. His explanation?

He was speeding because he was running late for a speed awareness course.

I am not entirely surprised that the Central Motorway Police Group tweeted about the stoppage with the hashtag #wordsfailme.

No less incredible was the excuse of the defence solicitor who arrived half an hour late. Asked to explain, he said:

"I have travelled here by car, and due to the fact that it is raining and my brake pads are worn, I have had to drive slowly."

And incredible is hardly adequate to describe one

defendant, as dispassionately described by the judge sentencing him:

"You were communicating with a person whom you believed to be a 14-year-old girl called Eva who was living in Germany... You made arrangements with her for you both to meet at Ashford International railway station. You discussed with her how you wanted to have sexual intercourse with her and how you would then kill her with an axe and eat her... you purchased an axe in Broadstairs and later photographed yourself holding the axe in your bedroom. On the day upon which you had arranged to meet Eva, you travelled to Ashford International Station but happily no one arrived... You told the court that you had had fantasies about cannibalism since you were a child... You have shown no remorse and *indeed cannot understand why anyone should find your behaviour in any way abnormal or perverted, let alone criminal.*"

WTF...?

Judges in the Family Court have understandably become fed up with continually being accused of operating in secret, and the judgments in a lot of cases involving children are now published, in an anonymised form, on the Internet on a site called BAILII. (It stands for British And Irish Legal Information Institute, and is one of the finer examples of coining the acronym, then thinking of the words to fit it).

If you are publishing an anonymised version of a judgment, you obviously can't label it *Bloggs v Wafflesnook* or whatever, so these cases are known by faintly incomprehensible sets of initials; and one such is a case which you will find at http://www.bailii.org/ew/cases/EWCA/Civ/2009/358.html, officially rejoicing in the title of *CP v AR and another* [2009] EWCA Civ 358.

Lord Justice Wall, in the Court of Appeal, observed:

"...as I read the papers in the instant appeal, and, in particular, the report and the oral evidence of Professor Zeitlin, and listened to the careful arguments addressed to us, I was

powerfully reminded of the first four lines of
Philip Larkin's poem *This be the Verse*",

which I do not propose to quote here because I have
no desire to investigate the interesting legal question of
whether, in quoting Lord Justice Wall at greater length,
I would be expensively breaching the copyright of the
late Mr Larkin. But suffice it to say that large sections of
the Family Bar have mordantly re-christened the case
Re F.

In which connection, what may be thought to have
been research going above and beyond the call of duty
was undertaken by Mr Justice Bean in a 2011 case.

The Police had been looking for people who might
be in possession of cannabis. They found three young
men, including the defendant, and decided to search
them. "Fuck this, man, I ain't been smoking nothing,"
complained the defendant. He was searched. They
found nothing. "Told you, you won't find fuck all,"
said the defendant. The officer decided to see if any
of the group was wanted by the police, and asked the
defendant if he had a middle name. The reply – "No,
I've already fucking told you so." – led to an arrest
under section 5 of the Public Order Act, which resulted
in the defendant being fined £50. But the prosecution
had to prove not only the use of threatening, abusive
or insulting words, but that they were used within the
hearing of someone else who was caused or was likely
to have been caused harassment, alarm or distress by
hearing them.

Resignedly, Mr Justice Bean observed:

"A search on the legal database Lexis for cases in which either the word 'fuck' or the word 'fucking' appear produces 2,124 results. Even allowing for duplication in the way that cases are reported and transcribed, or for cases which appear in more than one report, the total is still very large. Fortunately [counsel] only found it necessary to cite six of the many cases which bear on this vexed topic."

He concluded that there was no evidence that either of the police officers had been caused or was likely to have been caused, harassment, alarm or distress as a result of the use of the f-word, and the expensively obtained conviction was quashed. As Lord Justice Glidewell had wisely observed in another case:

"...words and behaviour with which police officers will be wearily familiar will have little emotional impact on them save that of boredom."

The same words used by a Mr Fagan some years earlier proved more costly. He was parking his car under the instructions of a police officer, who asked him to park closer and indicated a precise spot. Mr Fagan drove forward towards him and stopped it with the offside wheel on P C Morris's left foot. "Get off, you are on my foot," said the officer. "Fuck you, you can wait," responded the appellant.

Although it is quite hard to point to anything that

Mr Fagan actually *did* which amounted to an assault, it will come as no surprise to learn that he was convicted of assaulting P C Morris. The Clerk of the Court in *The Wind in the Willows,* who scratched his nose with his pen and observed:

> "Some people would consider that stealing the motor-car was the worst offence; and so it is. But cheeking the police undoubtedly carries the severest penalty; and so it ought. Supposing you were to say twelve months for the theft, which is mild; and three years for the furious driving, which is lenient; and fifteen years for the cheek, which was pretty bad sort of cheek, judging by what we've heard from the witness-box…"

would have approved.

The same expletive got counsel into a lot of hot water in a case involving the obligation to restore parts of South Wales that had been used for coal mining. The landowners were contemplating transferring the land to a company based in the British Virgin Islands and were anxious to know whether they would be left with the obligations to restore the land. Counsel wrote an opinion saying that they would; and then, having negotiated a rather tasty fee for doing so, wrote a second opinion saying that they would not. In the course of an ill-fated and very expensive attempt to prosecute the directors and lawyers for conspiracy to defraud, as the judge related:

"The Crown relies upon a statement from [counsel's] clerk who, upon being told of the size of the fee for the second opinion negotiated by [counsel] personally declares:

'Fuck me, that's a serious amount of money.'

That, it is said, is the clearest evidence that the fee was much more than anything that could be described as commercial."

Be that as it may, Mr Justice Hickinbottom concluded that the objective was lawful, the means used to achieve it were lawful, and that conspiring to do something lawful by lawful means could not be an offence. Which is why I don't name counsel.

SHOOT THAT SPELL-CHECKER!

There are some Funnies which traditionally tend to get reproduced under the heading of "Shoot that typist!" but it is probably fairer to blame modern spell-checking software. If the word which is typed by mistake is a valid word in the dictionary, a spell-checker will not flag it up as an error. This is a particular problem with the words "NOW" and "NOT" which sometimes get exchanged, with devastating consequences for the sense of the document.

The problem of the Typo affects everyone. One senior appeal judge made an excellent speech which as originally reported referred to:

"outbursts of pubic disapprobation."

And dressing to the other side, as it were, when the footballer Adam Johnson was on trial, the *Independent* reported his long-suffering girlfriend as giving evidence that she had

"never seen his public area shaved".

Famously a draft lease once recited that the (exorbitant) rent was so many thousand pounds

"per anum".

The tenant's solicitor probably enjoyed being able to observe, deadpan:

"It is through the nose that our client is paying."

The Curse of the Spell-Checker explained, if it did not, perhaps, excuse, the application to vary a contact order

"…as the current arrangements do not fit in with the father's shit pattern.",

as also the legend which appeared carefully typed at the foot of every letter going out from one colleague's former firm:

"The office will be shit between 24th and 27th December…"

Exactly the same Curse resulted in a Defendant's solicitors writing to inform the court that

"The Claimant's drat directions are agreed."

A sentiment with which the District Judge probably agreed. I rather like the direction proposed by a well-known firm of insurance lawyers that:

"...the Court list this matter for a case management conference at the first opportunity having first advised the parties of the need to file Directions Questionnaires and proposed Draft *Depredations*."

Some who are ill-disposed to the insurance industry would see a certain aptness there.

Even being polite to your correspondent has its hazards. One solicitor wrote a careful and polite email to his opponents explaining why he thought their approach to a matter had been mistaken, and that their claim not to have received a particular letter of his would have been more convincing had they not actually replied to it at one stage. "Regards," he wrote, before hitting the 'send' button – realising just too late that he had in fact written: "Retards".

★ ★ ★

Make precisely what you will of the alleged complaint by a wife petitioner:

"The Respondent demanded annual intercourse"

or of the letter received in a case about children explaining that the mother had been involved in an incident on the street, in which she had been

"pushed and shaved".

And in another case the court was informed that one of the parents had an alcohol problem and it was suggested that the court order a

"lover function test."

Mediation is, justifiably, a recommended approach for dealing with many family matters. One typist, however, possibly displayed more accuracy than she knew when she suggested (apparently on more than one occasion) that certain of the firm's clients were

"suitable for medication."

We have all met them...

As well as spell-checkers, of course, modern word-processors offer the marvellous timesaver that is Autotext. I never have to type out "District Judge" in full, having primed my computer to know what "DJ" means. Granted, I may be in difficulties if I ever have to try a case involving a mobile discotheque. But I sympathise with the colleague who spent most of his time trying crime, but found himself considering some family law legislation embodied in the form of a Statutory Instrument, or SI. His computer had been informed that SI was a time-saving abbreviation for Sexual Intercourse.

At least autotext had not been invented when, many years ago, a colleague was asked to provide a copy of his notes for the hearing of an appeal.

He had carefully annotated what he thought were two killer points made by one of the advocates.

He received an urgent note from the High Court judge hearing the appeal:

> Your notes are very clear and helpful. But could you help me with the abbreviation OSM!!?

Let us just say that he did not admit that the abbreviation actually stood for

> "Oh, Shit! Moment!!"

From the same period came a story of the Land Charges Registry, at that time uncomputerised and not noted for its efficiency. For reasons which were apparently perfectly sound, a hapless solicitor was attempting to make a search against the name of R. B. Jones. The clerk at the Land Charges Registry, no doubt mindful of the Registry's less than stellar reputation, sent the application form back seeking clarification. The solicitor, becoming exasperated, returned it, asking for a search against R(only) B(only) Jones.

A search certificate duly materialised. Against the name of Ronly Bonly Jones.

AND BEWARE OF CUT AND PASTE

Naturally, a lot of documents we see in court contain chunks of fairly standard text. That is a sensible approach in many cases. But what do you make of the claim for car hire charges after a road accident which included a recital that

> "…the Claimant had been deprived of the use of the vehicle for shopping, social outings in the evening and taking children to and from school."

Perfectly reasonable? In many cases, but probably not where *the car was a panda car and the claimant was the Chief Constable.*

Perhaps, by analogy with cut-and-shut, cut-and-paste is particularly prevalent in matters to do with vehicles. But even that hardly excuses one set of particulars of claim which solemnly asserted:

> "The Claim arises as a result of a Road Traffic Accident".

So far so commonplace, but…

"The Defendant is a social landlord. The Claimant was walking down a tiled slope in the garden area of the Defendant's premises when she slipped and fell."

★ ★ ★

And in a mortgage possession list, an affidavit of evidence duly recited:

"The claimant has attempted to reach an agreement with the defendant for clearance of the arrears on the mortgage account but has been unable to do so."

That was unsurprising given that in answer to the inquiry 'What information is known about the defendant's circumstances?' appeared the words:

"The defendant is deceased."

HEAR, HEAR

Audio typists are clever people, and the people who design voice recognition software to cope with the English language are, perhaps, even cleverer, but sometimes crucial words are misheard.

Thus, at the end of a long and aggrieved fax from Mother's solicitors, solemnly intending to fawn in the usual way over the *'honourable* court' (readers are referred to the discussion of 'with respect' on page 24):

> "We would ask the *horrible* Court to take the contents of this letter into account when considering the Father's application."

Slightly less embarrassingly, another firm of solicitors had managed to agree the amount of the damages with their opponents and, again intending to fawn on the court by *respectfully* asking that the hearing be shortened, wrote:

> "…we restfully request that…"

But as the District Judge (me), who would otherwise have had to spend two hours listening to tedious argument over the appropriate level of the damages, was able to confirm, the request was indeed, in one sense, "restful".

To what sort of judge should the application be referred? According to one solicitor who may have thought the judge learned but whose typist evidently didn't,

"a learner District Judge".

What had caused the accident in the first place? Possibly, as one colleague read with surprise,

"The Defendant pulled out in front of the bus causing the bus to break."

A probation officer compiling a pre-sentence report for the Magistrates probably did not intend to confirm that the defendant had returned to running his own business and would be able to get on with work

"as soon as he had retrieved his belongings from the porn shop"

any more than the author of a Cafcass (welfare service) report in another case meant to inform the court that

"Abdul's school attendance in recent months has become increasingly erotic."

I shall refrain from comment. You can make up your own. Young Abdul's problems were doubtless comparable to those of the young man who was described as suffering from

"Attention Defecate Hyperactive Disorder"

and whose case would presumably have been an appropriate home for the observation contained in another Cafcass report:

"There is no doubt that the relationship between ------'s parents is stained."

As, no doubt, was the relationship between the couple, one of whom in answer to an application for an injunction offered the reassurance that he was now taking "beater-blockers".

Another family relationship may have been in the judge's mind when His Honour Judge Leonard heard an application to halt a complex criminal trial because suitable defence advocates could not be found at the rates the Legal Aid authorities were willing to pay. The case was argued on behalf of the defendants by Alexander Cameron QC, brother of one David. Outlining the arguments which had been put to him, the judge recorded that Mr Cameron had appeared bro bono.

This was, of course, a typo for the expression *pro bono*, short for *pro bono publico*, meaning that a lawyer acts without fee because the cause is a deserving one. But understandably it attracted the mischievous comment in the pages of the *Law Society's Gazette*:

> "…we think it translates loosely as 'sticking one on your brother for the public good'."

When in practice, one colleague recalled dictating an offer letter to a firm of insurers which was meant to read: "my client will accept £5000 in general damages". By what can only be described as a cock up, this came out as:

> "my client will accept £5000 in genital damages."

A young man featured in a case in my list because he had been using his council flat for growing and selling cannabis. The Council's solicitors had carefully completed the claim form stating:

> "The following is known about the defendant's circumstances. Mr ---- suffers from ADHD, gross dyslexia and has asparagus."

Takes one to know one, I believe the saying is.

The solicitor in a divorce case, proposing the formal *dismissal* of his client's claims (a form of tying up loose ends of family finance) may have been surprised to find that he had actually written:

> "Please find enclosed Form A for *dismal* purposes only."

Another solicitor drafting particulars of the Respondent's behaviour evidently had a typist who was a Harry Potter fan:

> "In 2010 the Respondent [falsely] claimed to have been *muggled* on his way home from work."

★ ★ ★

You need to explain why the court has jurisdiction to deal with your case, commonly because the Petitioner is *habitually resident* in England. Not, as another hapless lawyer found he had asserted of his client:

> "The Petitioner is domiciled and *a bitch actually resident* in England and Wales."

Having established that the court had jurisdiction, another solicitor went on in his client's petition to complain of

> "… the Respondent's jackal and hide behaviour…",

about which another judge sardonically commented:

> "How can the petition possibly succeed? The Respondent has a wild dog, but is careful to hide it from the Petitioner. Clearly, the actions of a responsible dog owner or zoo keeper. I'd dismiss the petition summarily."

★ ★ ★

A colleague was surprised to read a long submission about the *Civil* Procedure Rules, written by a solicitor, referring several times to the

"Seville Procedure Rules".

As he observed: "Creeping European influence?" Or, as someone else suggested, a recipe for marmalade. But the *mot juste* was undoubtedly the response:

"It's a codification of the old common law Spanish Practices."

In the course of the argument between a Mr and Mrs Calderbank about their matrimonial finances, one of them made an offer to settle the proceedings. The other rejected the offer but didn't secure a better result and, as the rules then stood, got penalised in costs. *Calderbank* letters duly became standard procedure. But the solicitors may have been stating no more than the truth when they included in counsel's instructions the statement that

"…the other side had sent a *'Call the Bank* letter'."

Presumably, observed counsel, the Manager had not made any counter offer.

★ ★ ★

Payments may be made *ex gratia* – without legal obligation. To describe such a payment as

"...an *excretia* payment..."

may give the wrong impression, as did the remarkable letter received by one colleague while at the Bar which, in seeking to thank her for her *assistance*, actually said:

"We write to thank you for *arsefisting* us last week..."

Not, however, as wrong as the reference to the doctrine of *res ipsa loquitur* (a grand-sounding statement of the obvious which literally and accurately translates as 'the thing speaks for itself'):

"The Claimant will rely on the doctrine of *raised hips locked together*."

When resisting an application for summary judgment (see page 165) it may be necessary to show that there is a *triable* issue; not, as one judge had offered to him when in practice, a "*tribal* issue".

The same judge recalled fondly a defendant for whom he acted in an accident claim. The defendant had been required by his insurers to attend to give evidence, but he had a protected no-claims discount, no excess and no personal injury [this was before whiplash became the country's biggest growth industry] and therefore no financial interest in the outcome. He considered himself completely *blameless*, but...

"My instructions read that he was angry at having to attend as he considered that he was completely brainless. The solicitors turned out to be much nearer the mark than they realised."

Well, after the hearing, the issue will have been decided, or, to use the weary Latin tag, *res judicata*. And should anyone try to re-litigate it, it will not be necessary, as one typist with no Latin suggested, to "…rely on the principle of *Raise Judy Carter…*"

THOU SHALT COMMIT [2]
ADULTERY...

Adultery in the divorce courts no longer involves evidence from chamber-maids that reads like a bad novel. But even in the 21st century there is a certain pleasure in reading in a divorce petition that

> "The Respondent has committed adultery with a *gentleman* whom it is not intended to name."

And an equal pleasure in finding as respondent to an uncontested adultery petition someone rejoicing in the name of "Fidelity".

Another adultery petition followed the husband coming home unexpectedly and finding the wife in bed with a 'strange' man. The Acknowledgment of

---

2   Our modern misfortunes with spell-checkers and bad proof reading pale into insignificance beside the fate of Robert Barker and Martin Lucas, the royal printers in London, who in 1631 produced what was meant to be a reprint of the King James Bible, but which omitted one crucial word from the Seventh Commandment in Exodus 20:14. Charles I was outraged and the Star Chamber punished the unfortunate Barker and Lucas severely. It was left to the next King Charles to elevate "Thou shalt commit adultery" into an art form.

Service form invites the respondent to say whether the adultery is admitted. The wife in this case, confronted with the question "Do you admit the adultery alleged in the petition?", came up with the memorable reply:

"Yes. So what…"

Another District Judge reminisced:

"I remember acting for a client who, when asked to complete that section of the acknowledgment, and having had a very difficult relationship for some years with his former wife, asked if he could put 'yes - and I really enjoyed it'."

With an uncharacteristically straight face, she added: "I thought it was best to discourage him."

MORE ABOUT MARRIAGE

One District Judge of my acquaintance reflected on what six years on the Bench had taught him about marriage. Some of his more repeatable thoughts included:

"Never marry a taxi driver. They earn nothing unless they are fortunate to have a whiplash injury which boosts their income...

Many women who have not been in paid work for years do not realise how employable they are after divorce. They can easily get a highly paid job a couple of weeks after decree absolute. This must be right as so many men say so."

The affidavit of evidence in another case recited, coining a neologism that may have been nearer the truth than was comfortable, that

"The parties continue to share a bed in the cramped, one bedroom bungalow but this is purely *plutonic*..."

while another District Judge recalled a case from when he was in practice

> "...where my client, the wife, assured me nothing could happen as the pyjama cord had been double knotted."

Strange. I'd always assumed that the colloquialism 'get knotted!' had precisely the opposite implication. But what do I know?

★ ★ ★

Seeking to dissolve the marriage presents its dilemmas to the conscientious professional. Thus, an item seen in a solicitor's bill of costs:

> "Consideration of ethics of booking the Respondent as a strip-o-gram to make him available for service as process servers had encountered great difficulty in completing service."

Or an extract from an affidavit of attempted service, which might also appear in the section about spell-checkers:

> "[X] informed me... that he has also sent a written notice of the proposed ex parte application to the First Defendant and left a massage for her with a gentleman who

answered her mobile phone. The gentleman refused to disclose his name [as well he might] but promised to pass on the massage to her."

In 2014, the High Court was confronted with nearly two hundred Italian couples who, for reasons which no doubt seemed good to them, wished to be divorced in England. The procedure they adopted involved fraud on a truly industrial scale. As the President of the Family Division put it, petitions were issued in 137 different county courts

> "...ranging, alphabetically from Aldershot to York and geographically across the length and breadth of England and Wales, from Truro in south-west England to Canterbury in south-east England, Haverfordwest in south-west Wales, Llangefni in north-west Wales, Carlisle in north-west England and Newcastle in north-east England."

Now, as you will recall from a few pages back, for the English courts to have jurisdiction, the petitioner needed to be habitually resident in England and Wales. And 179 petitioners solemnly informed various courts that they lived at Flat 201, 5 High Street, Maidenhead.

That would have been fairly surprising even had it been true. But that it was *not* true was demonstrated in startling fashion. Continued the President:

"On 28 August 2012, police officers of the Thames Valley Police executed a search warrant in relation to Flat 201. The evidence of one of the officers who executed the search warrant, Detective Sergeant Steven Witts of Thames Valley Police, whose witness statement is dated 4 March 2014, confirms that Flat 201 was not a residential property or, indeed, a property capable of occupation. It was in fact a mail box, mail box 201, one of a number of mail boxes located in commercial premises. As the investigating officer in charge of the police investigation, Detective Sergeant Jonathan Groenen, mordantly commented in his witness statement dated 29 October 2013, 'It is not possible for 179 applicants or respondents to reside at this address.' *Indeed, given the dimensions of the mail box it is clear that not even a single individual, however small, could possibly reside in it.*"

And 180 decrees of divorce were duly set aside.

AND MORE ABOUT SEX

A defendant, charged under section 66 of the Sexual Offences Act 2003 with pleasuring himself in public, was not present when the case was called on. His solicitor came into court to offer an explanation:

Solicitor: Your Worships, I apologise for the absence of the defendant. He's just called me to explain that he'll be a bit late as he couldn't get his car to start, but now he's coming on the bus.

Quick-witted Chairman of the Bench: Isn't he in enough trouble already?"

This prompted a retired District Judge to recall a course where trainee Recorders (part-time Circuit Judges) were dealing with a test case of indecent assault. One of his colleagues informed the class that

"…he would have dismissed the case 'willy-nilly'."

And another colleague reminisced about a

"...solicitor complaining in a buggery case before the local magistrates that until the prosecution produced the committal papers he couldn't get to the bottom of the case."

Then there was the Leeds barrister mitigating for a client who had pleaded/been found guilty of doing unspeakable things with a horse:

"He now has a girlfriend. They have a stable relationship."

I was once told that many years ago a resident of the little Bedfordshire village of Elstow (birthplace of John Bunyan) was alleged to have committed an unnatural offence with a sheep, and admitted that he had, indeed, done so. The village bobby (I told you it was many years ago) is said to have questioned the individual concerned:

Policeman: Now, was this a male sheep or a female sheep?

Accused (indignantly): A female sheep, of course. What do you take me for, a pervert?

MARRIAGE À LA MODE…?

Hindsight is, of course, a wonderful thing, but the judge reading a petition referring to a marriage celebrated at 'A Very Special Memory Wedding Chapel, Las Vegas' can be forgiven a wry smile on noting that the petition was issued a year and a day after the marriage.

And what exactly does one make of this:

"The Petitioner and Respondent first met in 2003 and married on 10th January 2004 *due to the Respondent's unreasonable behaviour*" ?

Do I really have the power to order the matrimonial home contents to be chopped up and scattered on the Leeds United pitch?

Speaking of behaviour, the particulars of behaviour included in a petition sometimes make very sad reading. Thus (and please bear in mind that the following actually happened):

> "The Respondent is completely obsessed with the game of Cricket. He plays the game every Saturday and Sunday as well as on weekday evenings. When he isn't playing he watches the game on TV. In an effort to save the marriage the Petitioner persuaded the Respondent to attend Relate. The Relate Counsellor suggested that the parties consider pursuing some shared activity and to this end the parties purchased bicycles with a view to taking country rides together. On the occasion of the first cycle outing the parties passed a cricket ground where a match was in progress. The Respondent noticed that one of the teams was a man short so he turned his bike around and went home to collect his whites before joining the game; the Petitioner then concluded that the marriage was at an end."

By the way, never let it be said that the judiciary overlook the possibility of unconscious bias. The District Judge in whose paperwork this appeared admitted to being a cricket buff and passed the file to a colleague to deal with.

Perhaps it's best not to think too hard about the following, which turned up in my paperwork one day:

"I do not accept that the grounds for the breakdown of the marriage was as a result of my unreasonable behaviour. Indeed, the Petitioner has indicated that I was convicted of attempted murder. This is incorrect and I was convicted of grievous bodily harm. I was originally charged with attempted murder but the charge was reduced to Section 18 Grievous Bodily Harm with intent to harm. The reason why the marriage broke down was because of the Petitioner's adultery with my best friend... I do not consider that the breakdown of the marriage was anything to do with my behaviour. The reason for the violence was because the Petitioner advised me that she had been committing adultery."

While obviously I found it difficult to understand anyone cuckolding such a paragon, that Petitioner got her divorce. As did the one who

"... called into the matrimonial home during the day and found the Respondent sitting behind his desk with no trousers or underpants on. His secretary was in the same room kneeling on the floor and refusing to look the Petitioner in the eye. The Respondent's explanation was that it was more comfortable for him to work like that on hot days and that his secretary did not object."

Another one for the collector of unbelievable particulars of behaviour:

> "The Petitioner was almost two weeks overdue when pregnant with the parties' son. The Petitioner attended hospital on the Thursday when she was informed by the doctor that she should be induced for labour the following day. The Respondent said that this would not be possible as he had tickets for a rugby match he wanted to attend on the Saturday. The doctor therefore agreed to induce the labour on the Monday instead. This caused the Petitioner to feel extremely distressed."

You don't say. You really don't say.
In another case

> "The Respondent handed over a box of the Petitioner's post marked 'to the life form formerly known as xxx'. The Petitioner found this disrespectful."

How thin skinned can you be?
One respondent was so unwise as to send a message to his spouse to the effect that seeing particulars of his behaviour set down in black and white "seemed a bit harsh". A few nanoseconds elapsed before the lady fired back:

> "You shouldn't have been such a twat, then."

Some people do learn from their mistakes, but not our hero, who, in the course of discussions about money, expressed the concern that his ex might be going to cohabit. Back came the prompt reply:

> "Never mind about cohabiting; after 18 months of living with you, I think I am questioning my sexuality."

To show your are cohabiting with this man, your husband must prove 'a shared daily life, stability, and a degree of permanence' – well, they'll never succeed on 'stability'

Occasionally, extreme facts in a matrimonial case used not to be enough. Thus the reminiscence of one judge, recalling a case heard by the redoubtable Mr Justice Wrangham (whom we shall meet again in a different context on page 130), before they reformed the divorce law in 1970:

"Each spouse had petitioned/cross-petitioned on the grounds of cruelty. After 10 days of evidence – silk on both sides, all on Legal Aid – His Lordship expressed the view that each had got what they deserved and given as good as they got, and left the unhappy couple firmly wedded to each other."

Even after the divorce law was reformed, Mr Justice Bagnall felt able in late 1971 to express the view that:

"...if I may give a few examples, it seems to me that a violent petitioner can reasonably be expected to live with a violent respondent; a petitioner who is addicted to drink can reasonably be expected to live with a respondent similarly addicted; a taciturn and morose spouse can reasonably be expected to live with a taciturn and morose partner; a flirtatious husband can reasonably be expected to live with a wife who is equally susceptible to the attractions of the opposite sex; and if each is equally bad, at any rate in similar respects, each can reasonably be expected to live with the other. This conclusion seems to me to be consonant with what have been said to be the objects of the 1969 legislation which are not, in my view, simply to make divorce easier."

The reformed divorce law, of course, controversially introduced the idea of divorce on the grounds of separation – two years' separation and the consent of the parties suffices. It is widely overlooked that as virtually no divorce case ever goes to a hearing, undefended divorces being dealt with on paper, an immediate divorce by consent is available if one spouse is prepared *to state that* s/he has committed adultery and the other is prepared *to state that* s/he finds it intolerable to live with the self-proclaimed adulterer. As noted at page 83, these days nobody calls the chambermaid to check.

Divorce on the grounds of separation still leaves the possibility of the occasional jaw-dropping revelation, because in the affidavit asking for the divorce the Petitioner used to be invited to indicate the reason for the separation. First prize in that competition must go to the Petitioner in one seaside County Court whose answer was:

"I came home early from sea and found my wife in the hallway at the foot of the stairs with her tights and panties in one hand and two £20 notes in the other. She obviously didn't see it was me because she said, 'If you want it we'd better be quick, Jim, because I think I heard my husband's car in the road'. I walked out and haven't seen her since."

Far preferable to attempted murder or GBH, it must be admitted.

★ ★ ★

One question in the statement which the petitioner has to complete to obtain the decree nisi on the basis of the respondent's behaviour asks whether the respondent's behaviour has affected the petitioner's health. This does not appear to have any obvious purpose – I suspect that the reason for the question may be that "unreasonable behaviour" replaced the old ground of divorce known as "cruelty", proving which did require the petitioner to show that his/her health had been affected. But no doubt the musings of one of the Family Division District Judges are correct:

Q. What difference would any reply make to our decision to grant or refuse a certificate of entitlement to decree nisi?

A. None. Except if the reply was: I felt a lot better than normal after the behaviour. Whereupon I would refuse the decree.

★ ★ ★

The real dispute in these cases is usually over money, and one District Judge had a case in which the wife was a clairvoyant with syndicated fortune telling columns in a number of newspapers and magazines.

> "Her solicitor said that she does have a substantial income, 'but who knows what the future holds?' I refrained from suggesting the answer."

The Petitioner in another set of proceedings certainly had a way with words:

> "The Respondent visited prostitutes and acquired pornographic videos. He also smoked large quantities of cannabis. That is what he means when he talks about our joint debts."

Or, as the Respondent in yet another case claimed, perhaps implying that it had all been a bad dream:

> "I paid all the debts during the mirage."

He thought of himself as an income stream, but she thought of him more as an estuary

THE DOCTOR HAS ORDERED...

Do you take medical reports at face value? Sometimes you shouldn't. A medical report on a 5-year-old claimant read:

> "Has photo ID been checked? Yes. What type of ID? Photo driving licence."

All right, that probably referred to the child's parent's driving licence, but how do you explain the statement

> "She was able to get out of the car unaided"

referring to a 9 month old baby? As the District Judge who received this nonsense, and was the mother of twins, observed: "I must have strong words with my, nearly 12 months olds, they are obviously capable of much more than they are letting on."

And counsel might have done well to engage brain in gear before opening mouth in a tripping case in which the doctor's report commented, "typical football injury".

Counsel solemnly, in line with positive instructions

from the insurers, put it to the claimant that that was the cause – playing a fierce game of soccer. He did not get far. The claimant in question was a somewhat frail woman, 75 years of age.

And in another accident claim, the claimants were seeking compensation for "whiplash" injuries including lower back pain. They produced a report from someone I could describe as a 'tame doctor' which recited that there were no other conditions which might explain the lower back pain allegedly experienced by Mr and Mrs C at the time of his examination.

For reasons with which I need not trouble you, the claimants were subsequently examined by the insurers' not quite so tame doctor, who dryly made what you may consider a reasonable observation:

"I would have expected Dr --- to observe that Mrs C was 8½ months pregnant at the time of his examination."

UNPARLIAMENTARY LANGUAGE

Some pieces of legislation appear to have a remarkable capacity for disabling common sense. Probably the worst offender is the Data Protection Act, which gave rise to the following absurdity quoted by Gerald Kaufman MP:

> "...the case of someone who had his phone stolen and when he asked for the numbers which the thief had dialled he was told he could not be given that information because of the Data Protection Act."

★ ★ ★

Frequently unfairly traduced, but occasionally the cause of spectacular foolishness, is that worthy piece of legislation, the Health and Safety at Work etc. Act 1974.

It was probably the excuse for what was reported from one magistrates' court:

> "We've had magistrates who are wheelchair users, one of whom was told that she couldn't

leave her electric wheelchair outside the courtroom because it was a hazard."

Another fine example of the sort of box-ticking idiocy which arouses the ire of *Daily Mail* leader writers is offered by a former District Judge from Devon:

> "When I was in the old Torquay County Court in a converted cottage hospital near the town centre, as opposed to the present palais de justice, every few months someone would attend to test the strength of the ring in the wall intended for a rope for my escape in the event of fire. He would happily tick the box to satisfy Health & Safety that all was well. It never occurred to him that (a) there was no rope and (b) the windows were hermetically sealed and of toughened glass – to prevent attempted suicide, I assume – and the room was on the second floor of the building."

Palais de justice, eh? I may just have been unfortunate (and, however unfair on Milton Keynes, some would so describe visiting both Milton Keynes and Luton in the same lifetime) but it has been my experience that if you have a magistrates' court and a county court in the same town it will always be the county court which occupies the nondescript concrete shoebox and the magistrates' court which luxuriates in the marble faced p de j. However…

At another county court, there is a 'tea point' with a kettle, though no tea and no running hot water. And no soap or washing up liquid. One visiting judge learned the reason:

> "...they carried out a risk assessment and thought that washing up liquid was too dangerous in case the Judges and Magistrates drank it by mistake."

At this point I must swallow hard and recount an unfortunate, but completely true, tale concerning the judges' tea-making equipment at the old Bletchley & Leighton Buzzard County Court, which used to be housed in one of the 'huts' at Bletchley Park. Curiously, given the provenance of the building, security at this establishment was, shall we say, not very tight.

> One of the Registrars (as District Judges were then known) evidently managed to get seriously up the nose of a litigant who determined to take a terrible revenge.
>
> Came the lunch break, Registrar retreated to his room and switched the kettle on with a view to a nice refreshing cup of tea. As the kettle warmed up, an aroma of something that certainly was not P G Tips filled the room.
>
> Close inspection revealed that a large, fresh human turd had been deposited within the kettle.

That was in the dear, departed days before 'Elf 'n' Safety, but the Registrar settled for a glass of tap water that day.

I'm not allowed to fire a rifle in case it damages my hearing!

★ ★ ★

In fact, there *is* a risk, and indeed a risk to Health and Safety, from liquids in the courts, but it tends to be overlooked. Many people wish to bring bottles of water into the court with them. You may feel that this seems reasonable enough. The air conditioning tends to dry the throat, and people are often nervous anyway. The risk arises if the clear liquid in the bottle turns out not to be water. In one case at Cambridge County Court in 2010 it turned out to be petrol, and the disgruntled litigant had also had the foresight to equip himself with some matches.

Cambridge court did get repaired, though, unlike Hemel Hempstead County Court, which fortuitously caught fire some years ago at a time when (a) someone was seeking to conceal the fact that funds had been misappropriated; and (b) the Lord Chancellor's Department was anxious to close the court anyway.

★ ★ ★

Not infrequently, the target of the court's ire is the Parliamentary draftsman rather than the organisation trying to make sense of his work. Thus Lord Justice Sedley in *Roe v Sheffield City Council* (2004):

"The composition of [s 55 of the Tramways Act, 1870] may not have been the brightest jewel in the crown of Lord Thring's Parliamentary Counsel Office, but it says plainly enough that anyone who is injured because of the promoter's failure to comply with the law is to have a remedy. Picked over, as it has sedulously been by counsel, it comes apart. But all that is then left, as Mr Maxwell [counsel for the tramway company] and Mr Sales [counsel for the Secretary of State for Transport] contentedly accepted, is a section which says that where there is liability there is liability. I do not think Parliament was wasting time and ink on such vacuities."

Sedley again, in *Irving v Commissioners of HMRC* (2004), taking a well-deserved swing at section 595 of the Income and Corporation Taxes Act 1988:

"Not for the first time, we have had to go to Bannockburn by way of Brighton Pier. This is not how legislation should be written."

Travel, even if not to Bannockburn, presents its own problems for the Parliamentary Draftsman. One Government lawyer recalled that early in his career he had drafted the Railways (Penalty Fares) Regulations 1994:

"I drafted them, and then was promptly 'done' for a penalty fare on the day they came into force. And to make matters worse, the ticket collector then offered me a leaflet to explain."

Expensively in a different way, Sir Thomas Bingham in 1995, being less than enthusiastic about the Landlord and Tenant Act 1987, commented:

> "As it is, the legal profession would appear to be the main beneficiary of this obscure statute."

English land law, however, manages plenty of obscurity without the assistance of Parliament. Thus Oliver Cromwell:

> "English land law is a tortuous and ungodly jumble"

and Lord Macnaghten, described as 'the greatest of the equity lawyers who became Lords of Appeal':

> "...nobody by the light of nature ever understood an English mortgage of real estate."

Returning to the efforts of the Parliamentary draftsman, one should note the barbed comment of Lord Diplock in a 1968 case:

> "I... would gladly shirk this uncongenial task, but in the conflict of judicial opinion about this perspicuous legislation [the unlamented Selective Employment Payments Act 1966, long repealed] it would be pusillanimous not to stand up and be counted."

Lord Justice Diplock, by the way, was a fine lawyer given to the use of long words but with the self-awareness to comment on one of his own judgments that it was

"...widely thought to be a typical example of gratuitous philological exhibitionism."

Sometimes the draftsman's meaning is clear, but not necessarily what you might expect. Thus the Vagrancy Act, 1824, refers to a man "wilfully, openly, lewdly, and obscenely exposing his Person...". In 1970 a Mr Evans left his trousers undone in a manner which was certainly intended to be insulting – the woman who was the object of his activities had been treated to an unwanted view of the Evans penis a few months previously, for which he had duly been convicted – but on this occasion the bits of Evans which were on display did not include that one. Surprisingly, you may think, his appeal succeeded, as the Divisional Court held that in the 1824 Act the word 'person' meant 'penis' and nothing else. Said Mr Justice Ashworth:

"It may be, as counsel for the appellant said, that it was the forerunner of Victorian gentility which prevented people calling a penis a penis, but however that may be I am satisfied in my own mind that it has now acquired an established meaning to the effect already stated. It is, I venture to say, well known amongst those who practise in courts that the word 'person' is so used over and over again."

With a certain mischievous relish, the late Sir Robert Megarry pointed out that Parliament wasn't always consistent in its usage, for the Food Hygiene Regulations 1955 (now regulation 8(c) of the Food Hygiene (Markets, Stalls and Delivery Vehicles) Regulations 1966) stipulated that anyone engaged in the handling of food must

> "...keep any open cut or abrasion on any exposed part of his person covered with a suitable waterproof dressing."

Indeed, regulation 8(a) stipulates that such an individual shall

> "...keep as clean as reasonably practicable all parts of his person which are liable to come into contact with the food."

YOU COULD HAVE
PHRASED THAT BETTER

The Law Reports contain a judgment of the Chancery Court of York on disciplinary proceedings against a clergyman who had an improper association with one of his parishioners. The judgment recorded the evidence given by various character witnesses; but praising him for his "'hands on' approach" seemed an unfortunate choice of words in the circumstances. (*In re King (2009)*)

Speaking of kings, the order of Mr Justice Haddon Cave granting permission for judicial review (a procedure in which counsel generally exchange *skeleton arguments* or summaries of their respective cases) in the 2013 case concerning the reburial of the bones of Richard III, actually directed

> The substantive hearing of these proceedings to be set down for hearing next term (estimate 1 day). Skeletons to be exchanged 1 week before the substantive hearing.

The draftsman of a witness statement in a "whiplash" claim might have been wise to think again:

"My sex life was affected. My lower back and neck would continue to hurt me. I did manage to get slightly back to normal some five months after the accident and this frustrated my partner as well as me. It did affect our relationship for a small period of time, *but we bounced back*."

Considerably less bouncy, indeed rather sad, was the statement in a divorce affidavit, in reply to the instruction 'state briefly the reason or the main reason for the separation':

"The Petitioner was in the navy and the parties drifted apart."

I had just warned him about the possibility of sequestration but I wonder if he many have misheard what I said

What do you make of the response of the defendant to a small claim between two telecommunications companies? The defence suggested that

> "…it is very sad the matter has come to court due to a breakdown in communications."

One District Judge recalled that

> "In my first ever mitigation before magistrates, I described my emotionally fragile and alcoholic client as a person who tended to keep his problems *bottled up*."

By the side of which the Solicitor in Leeds Magistrates' Court, mitigating on behalf of a regular female shoplifter as to why she should not be sent to prison, almost fails to qualify:

> "Your worships, my client is expecting a baby in 9 months' time."

He was in good company. For example, the solicitor mitigating for a kerb-crawler who said:

> "My client is a respectable man who does a lot of charity work and is always willing to go that extra mile."

Or the one acting for a man on his fourth conviction for drink driving who suggested that his client be sent on a Drink-Impaired Driver programme. Why would that be a good idea? Well, as the literature for the programme tells us that those who have committed five or more drink-drive offences are unsuitable for it, there was a perfectly sensible answer available to the solicitor. Sensible, anyway, by comparison with the deathless

"It would raise his spirits."

Or the one pleading for his client's Staffie not to be put down. He had indeed bitten a police officer but, said the advocate,

"...the present owner had not had him long and the incident had been a 'teething problem'."

Yet another solicitor, acting for a client whose doctor had diagnosed him with kleptomania, declared:

"When he feels the urge to steal, he takes something for it."

Yes, it's easily done. As witness the very experienced District Judge who wincingly reminisced that

"Without thinking, in dealing with an application by a claimant who was seeking the return of his property taken by the police in a raid, and which included a machine gun, I told the claimant that in issuing when he did, *he had jumped the gun.*"

Sticking with the firearms theme, an expert witness in another case ought to have thought more carefully before putting pen to paper. The claim was by a female employee for PTSD (post-traumatic stress disorder) damages against her building society employer following two armed robberies in quick succession. The psychiatric report stated that

> "...the claimant is likely to be affected by a number of *trigger events...*"

Not only advocates and expert witnesses are guilty of such unfortunate turns of phrase.

There was the probation officer compiling a pre-sentence report on a young man accused of theft from his employer who wrote that

> "...the defendant "had no problems with handling money",

or the social workers compiling an assessment in care proceedings:

> "Current testing of Mr and Mrs X's drug use remains negative for heroin. However, towards the end of the assessment, information from one of the assessors highlighted that the couple are using cannabis, which they have failed to share with workers."

Similarly, the local newspaper sub-editor who came up with:

"Youth arrested for arson after setting fire to haystack is bailed."

And the woman appearing before the beaks on a means enquiry. She had been paying every fortnight and then stopped. Why?

"I lost my job."

"Why didn't you tell us, rather than just stopping paying?"

"I didn't think to do so."

"What was your job, by the way?"

"Debt management."

And, by way of proof positive that magistrates are in every sense representative of the communities from which they are drawn, including the occasional ability to open mouth and insert foot:

The magistrates were satisfied that the defendant had a drink problem, and put him on a supervision order with an order to attend an alcohol misuse programme. The Chairman looked at the defendant severely.

"We are willing to give you this opportunity. But you really are in the Last Chance Saloon."

★ ★ ★

Such things occur outside the courtroom, too. A colleague recalled the pleasures of private practice:

> "After very lengthy correspondence with the owner of a restaurant whose septic tank was faulty and kept overflowing onto my client's land, he wrote saying 'I am having nothing further to do with this effluent which is now entirely in the hands of my solicitors.'"

This drew the slightly obvious retort:

> "Good to see a solicitor getting his hands dirty for his client."

★ ★ ★

On a somewhat different tack, an email received by counsel from a client prompted the admiring comment: "The finest amendment in the history of pleading". The client had produced a witness statement, and then had second thoughts:

> "Dear S---
>
> My state of health means I can find it difficult to articulate what I would like to say and even struggle to find the correct words to sufficiently express what I mean.

With this in mind, I have therefore replaced the word 'malevolent' with the words 'spiteful, malicious and executed without a sense of social responsibility or moral conscience'.

Kind regards…"

That, as they say, is telling 'em.

THE COURT HAS ORDERED…

If you receive an order from the court and it seems to make no sense, it may be sensible to check whether it has been correctly typed. Thus a colleague found the following on a file, which, as he observed, brightened up his day:

> "The Defendant should serve the doughnuts by ordinary first class post and they will be deemed served 2 days after posting."

As he commented:

> "Documents/doughnuts? Oh well, I suppose the claimant will get his just desserts."

Some courts still attempt to type orders up from handwritten notes which may, or may not, be legible. Whether that entirely explains the following specimen is open to debate:

> "Unless by… defendant sends to court a defence in accordance with R16.5(2)BCPR

setting out conusly, coherently in plain english the defendant's version of the accident the exosting defendnats will strandas struck out and claiamnt may enter judgement."

Yes, that is a reference to *plain English* in there.

★ ★ ★

London, of course, always feels the need to go one better. I am still trying to puzzle out what was intended by the following which emerged from the Central London County Court some years ago:

IT IS HEREBY ORDERED THAT...

2. The second to fourth defendants do not exist

3. The fifth Defendant is a cat

4. The first defendant do lodge pornographic photographs with the Court no later than 4pm [date].

One litigant in person came up with an inspired response to such inanities. He wrote:

"As I do not understand law, have no legal training, and am only very slightly conversant in legalese, I would request that all court documents be translated into English."

Sadly, the response is not recorded. But it is time to turn our attention to the bane of every judge's life – the documents produced by the parties.

It's modelled on a French system of pro-active case management, but 'heads of agreement' was translated as 'heads OFF agreement'!

IF IN DOUBT, COPY IT...

When my great-great-grandfather was involved in a case in Chancery in the early 19th century, everything had to be laboriously and very neatly copied out in immaculate copperplate. The work involved did cause people to think twice, and probably more than twice, before putting unnecessary documents before the court.

Since the advent of the photocopier, things have changed, and not for the better.

While on the Bench, Sir Stephen Sedley dryly summed up the situation in *Sedley's Laws of Documents*, which he has kindly allowed me to quote, observing, "These are the only laws which our profession invariably observes."

First Law: Documents may be assembled in any order, provided it is not chronological, numerical or alphabetical.

Second Law: Documents shall in no circumstances be paginated continuously.

Third Law: No two copies of any bundle shall have the same pagination.

Fourth Law: Every document shall carry at least three numbers in different places.

Fifth Law: Any important documents shall be omitted.

Sixth Law: At least 10 percent of the documents shall appear more than once in the bundle.

Seventh Law: As many photocopies as practicable shall be illegible, truncated or cropped.

Eighth Law: Significant passages shall be marked with a highlighter that goes black when photocopied.

Ninth Law:
    (a)   At least 80 percent of the documents shall be irrelevant.
    (b)   Counsel shall refer in court to no more than 10 percent of the documents, but these may include as many irrelevant ones as counsel or solicitor deems appropriate.

Tenth Law: Only one side of any double-sided document shall be reproduced.

Eleventh Law: Transcriptions of manuscript documents shall bear as little relation as reasonably practicable to the original.

Twelfth Law: Documents shall be held together, in the absolute discretion of the solicitor assembling them, by:
> a steel pin sharp enough to injure the reader,
> a staple too short to penetrate the full thickness of the bundle,
> tape binding so stitched that the bundle cannot be fully opened, or,
> a ring or arch-binder, so damaged that the two arcs do not meet.

Queen's Bench Master Ungley suggested two amendments:

Without prejudice to the Third Law, not less than five percent of documents shall be inserted in the bundle upside down.

Thirteenth Law: The bundle provided to the Court shall under no circumstances be identical to that in the hands of the advocates or to that provided to any witness.

Sedley did not mention the index, which is frequently one of the most irritating parts of the bundle. It tends to read something like this:

Case Summary – to follow
Chronology – to follow
Statement of issues – to follow

Other judges have tried a more subtle form of sarcasm. Thus Judge Behrens in 2014:

"Finally I would like to express my gratitude to Counsel for their clear and helpful submissions in a by no means straightforward case and for guiding me through a mass of documents which had been collated in such a way that any compliance with the Chancery Guide was coincidental."

Eventually, though, it was inevitable that one judge would decide he really had had enough. And in 2014, in a case which we shall encounter again in connection with the ridiculous costs which were incurred in it, Mr Justice Holman exploded:

"Having referred to the completely disproportionate costs that have been incurred, I turn now to the documentation which underlines the scale and intensity of this dispute. There were delivered to the court yesterday, or the day before, five large lever arch bundles of documents, which comprise over 2,000 pages, inclusive of the respective skeleton arguments, which are each just under 25 pages… As if that were not bad enough (as I will later describe), I was, frankly, flabbergasted this morning when the solicitors arrived at the court at about 10.10 am with another large cardboard box containing an additional five large lever arch files of additional documents (these are the ones with lavender coloured card on their spines). I have been told that those additional five bundles contain around a further 1,500 pages of documents. So, in aggregate, at the outset of this hearing, these parties are expecting consideration of all or part of 3,500 pages of documents... This needs to be considered within the framework that rule makers and the most senior judiciary have endeavoured to establish in order to ensure the proportionality of litigation...

'Unless the court has specifically directed otherwise, being satisfied that such direction is necessary to enable the proceedings to be disposed of justly, the bundle shall be contained in one [I emphasise the word, one]A4 size ring binder or lever arch file limited to no more than 350 sheets of A4 paper and 350 sides of text.'

A later 'statement', to which I will shortly refer, makes plain that the 350 sides of text must be inclusive, not exclusive, of the sides of paper in counsel's skeleton arguments.

Pausing there, one wonders, against the background of that clear practice direction, at how it could be that it is now contemplated that I should consider all or part of 3,500 pages of documents…

Except for the two skeleton arguments and the chronology, every single piece of paper that has so far been lodged will be taken away from this courtroom now…

I will adjourn this case now until 10.30 tomorrow morning. At 10.30 tomorrow morning, unless by then the parties have reached an overall settlement of this case, they must attend with one, single, composite bundle, containing not more than 300 pages as the President's direction requires. I say 300, for I am excluding and retaining the two existing skeleton arguments, which, as I have said, extend to about 50 pages…

If the parties cannot agree as to the contents of the documents bundle, then each side can select 150 pages of their own choosing, thereby making the total of 300."

Every single judge of my acquaintance who has read this judgment has laughed out loud at the quiet note that appears at the end of the report. Some have punched the air and exclaimed, "Yes!":

[NOTE: On the following morning the parties announced that they had reached a comprehensive settlement; and the judge was invited to make, and did make, an [order] in which their detailed agreement is contained in a confidential schedule.]

You may think that *Sedley's Laws* are a bit far-fetched. Well, where Sedley's Tenth Law is concerned, I have it on pretty good authority that on one occasion when the Court of Appeal was hearing an appeal, one of the Lords Justices was a little surprised to be approached by the clerk to one of the other members of the court.

"Could His Lordship borrow your papers, please?"

"I don't mind, of course, but why?"

"His papers only contain pages 1, 3, 5, 7 and 9 of the original judgment."

THE PERILS OF ADVOCACY

The first advice always given to an aspiring advocate is never to ask a question to which you do not know the answer.

Thus, it is said that the late Mr Justice Wrangham was once called to give evidence in the Magistrates' Court about a motor accident. Cross-examined by a certain inexperienced solicitor he was asked:

> "Come now, Sir Geoffrey: when you say you are certain that my client was driving at least at 60 mph what you really mean is that you *believe* he was driving at least at 60 mph."

> "Not so," replied his Lordship. "I am *certain* he was driving at least at 60 mph. I *believe* he was driving at 80 mph."

No doubt, whether it was 60 or 80, the motorist would nowadays be looking to hire a replacement car at an eye-watering daily rate. And sometimes the helpful strategy of the hire company comes badly unstuck. Thus, in what was aptly styled a fast track trial before a

Deputy District Judge, the answer to the first question put in evidence,

"Are the contents of your statement true?"

was

"No – it's what the man from the solicitors said I should say – but it isn't true."

The trial lasted about 15 seconds.

'So you want a Spot hire vehicle? No problem sir.'

The principle of not asking the question unless you know the answer held good in another case in which I had asked a welfare officer to try and find out about the wishes and feelings of a four year old child who was embroiled in a bitter battle between her parents. She reported that, invited to choose one to represent herself from a large selection of soft toys, the four-year-old chose (a) the smallest toy in the box which (b) was slightly damaged. At which point everyone in the room, and particularly both parents, looked very moved.

Thoughtfully and completely deadpan, the welfare officer added:

> "Perhaps I should have mentioned what she chose to represent the two of you"

> "Oh, what was that?" asked the parents, as one (falling for it completely).

> "Two fire-breathing dragons," came the devastating response.

It would have been pleasant to have been able to report that the parents' attitude to one another improved after that.

Sometimes the "question" doesn't even need to be articulated to leave the advocate flat on his back. The following exchange has been reported:

> Barrister, buttering up the expert witness: 'You seem like a man of probity and good character.'

Expert witness: 'If I were not under oath I would return the compliment.'

★ ★ ★

No, Molesworth. That is not what is meant by 'an abuse of process'

But sometimes, the advocate comes out on top. In a certain road traffic case, one issue was whether the driver of a Chelsea tractor which had shunted a much smaller vehicle from the rear, had, as alleged, informed the driver of the smaller car that he was "a lying twat".

"Certainly not," he declared. "I would never use language like that."

Three questions later, he indignantly challenged counsel for the claimant:

"Are you saying my car's a load of shit?"

Judgment for the Claimant, on that and other grounds.

★ ★ ★

One of the many black legal aphorisms that contain a germ of truth is the suggestion that

"Any lawyer who says he isn't interested in costs is either a liar, a ghost, or on a salary."

But even though counsel may be interested in costs (one aphorism that in my experience as a former solicitor contains no truth whatever is the one that asserts that "counsel are not concerned about money") their skill at dealing with the subject sometimes leaves something to be desired. Thus, at the end of a hearing, the judge had to "summarily assess" the costs of the successful party:

Counsel A (for paying party): 'I must say, Sir, that these costs seem extraordinarily high for such a straight forward application – gracious me, they come to nearly £2500!'

Counsel B (for receiving party): 'I think you are looking at your own costs schedule.'

Counsel A: 'Oh dear, so I am!'

In fairness, solicitor advocates sometimes have their own brand of awfulness in this field (and see, not entirely flippantly, at page 198). Back in the 1990s, at the end of a hearing where £3,000-odd had been claimed and £2,000 had been awarded:

Solicitor for Defendant: 'The Plaintiff's costs at £15,000 are outrageous. Please reduce them – but not below the £10,000 which we charged our client.'

After some quiet but pointed comments from the District Judge, the solicitors "asked for 5 minutes" – and agreed the amount of the costs.

★ ★ ★

The perils of advocacy do not, of course, begin when the advocate arrives at court. As one High Court Judge observed:

"I shan't forget elegant London counsel telephoning the Judge in Bury to explain his absence from there by his accidental presence in Bury St Edmunds. Keep the atlas in your chambers."

Though the problem may not be confined to the advocate. It is said that one Deputy District Judge eagerly reported for duty at Newport, Wales, to find that he was not well placed to deal with the list awaiting him at Newport, Isle of Wight.

The advocate's task may be made no easier by the material he is given to work with. As one District Judge resignedly commented:

"I have just seen a Trial bundle that has in the index the following: Page 104 Blank Document. Sure enough, turn to page 104 and there is a blank piece of paper not connected with the document that ends on page 103 or that which starts on page 105."

Even in the High Court, blanks may appear where they shouldn't. Thus a distinctly unimpressed Mr Justice Rimer in *Chester City Council v Arriva Plc* (2007):

"The third head of wasted expenditure, which came to the conveniently round figure of £1,000, was for various alleged outgoings. The figure was taken out of the air, it bore no relation to anything, and not a penny was made good. I reject this head of claim."

Not much better, one feels, was the brief which is said to have concluded:

> "Counsel will do all that he can to obtain an acquittal because the defendant is a friend of Princess Margaret, although instructing solicitors see with some surprise it is her sister who is prosecuting."

How did we manage before the advent of the Internet age and the expression <sigh>?

★ ★ ★

Apparently it was ever thus. Serjeant Sullivan, writing in the 1920s, summed up litigation in this way:

> "Before two parties embark on litigation they are perfectly well aware of what is at issue between them and what they each seek to prove. There is no reason whatever why, in a single document the moving party should not state his version of the dispute and serve it on his opponent, stamped with the seal of the Court calling on his opponent to answer it. There is no reason why his opponent should not be bound within a very short period to deliver his answer and forthwith let them go to trial.
>
> What in fact happens is that the Plaintiff serves a Writ which gives no information at all. It is quite useless and unnecessary. [Nowadays

we have a Claim Form. It serves the same purpose. And is often equally uninformative].

This is replied to by a document called 'entry of appearance' which gives no information and is quite unnecessary and useless. [We call it an Acknowledgment of Service these days].

There follows an application to a Master for directions. This is a device for making costs as what happens next is routine. In accordance with the 'directions' the Plaintiff then condescends to give his statement of claim. What he claims is never considered sufficient by any capable junior Counsel to whom the papers are sent to invent an application for further and better particulars, all unnecessary, expensive and prejudicial to the cause of justice. The Defence is served and Counsel uses his ingenuity in inventing applications for more and more particulars...

The County Court, which is sometimes called 'the poor man's court' emulates its professional big brother and in the High Court the enormous amount of papers which eventually constitute the Brief contains only a modest proportion of anything that Counsel would wish to know about the case. The rest serves its purpose in increasing costs...

The extraordinary thing is that it appears to be nobody's business to protect the community against the burden of legal costs."

A certain amount has changed in 90 years, but not as much as one might wish, though the courts have become a little firmer with what Sullivan accurately describes as "further and better particulars, all unnecessary, expensive and prejudicial to the cause of justice." These have been accurately parodied:

"It was agreed that Jack and Jill would climb the hill to fetch a pail of water."

"Of 'it was agreed' please state whether it was agreed orally or in writing. If it was agreed in writing, please provide a copy of the document or documents containing the agreement and please state on what date or dates the document or documents were entered into. If it was agreed orally please state when and where it was agreed, the identity of each of the participants taking part in the meeting and whom (if anyone) each participant represented. Please state the full terms of the agreement. Please state what was said by way of agreement by each of the participants taking part in the aforesaid meeting..."

THE VOICE OF EXPERIENCE

The three great lies are "The cheque is in the post", "My wife doesn't understand me" and "I'm from the UN and I'm here to help you", according to David Edgar in *The Prisoner's Dilemma*.

This was neatly parodied by Martin Bowley QC with the suggestion that:

> "The three great lies at the Bar are 'My brief said I wouldn't go down', 'My clerk said I could get here by 2 o'clock' and 'My accountant said it was allowable against tax'."

Counsel should perhaps not joke about tax, though. In 1954 Robert Megarry, later Sir Robert Megarry, Vice-Chancellor of the High Court, was prosecuted at the Old Bailey for submitting false income tax returns. Megarry earned money from lecturing, which his wife dealt with, and from practising at the Bar, dealt with by his clerk. Apparently wife and clerk each assumed that the other was dealing with certain items of income, but in fact neither did.

Tax credits have been great for us. Once John had mastered them, he found that qualifying as an accountant was child's play

The judge directed the jury to acquit Megarry, on the grounds that the error was a genuine mistake with no intention to defraud the tax authorities. Can't expect a senior chancery lawyer actually to read his tax return before signing it, after all.

Less fortunate was Rohan Pershad QC, who was jailed for three and a half years in February 2013 after being found guilty of VAT fraud, after "deliberately" not paying a total of £600,000 VAT over a period of 12 years.

IT'S CRIMINAL...

A leading family law judge told me the following, but I have heard it from other sources:

With a number of other part time judges he was sent on a training course dealing with crime. The regular criminal practitioners were somewhat over-free in discussing at the breakfast table the appropriate sentencing for various sexual offences. As he observed:

> "I'm all for having some sex – *but not with poached eggs!*"

In the same vein is the deadpan retort which, according to Evelyn Waugh, the incorrigible F. E. Smith (see page 2) gave to an inquiry from a High Court Judge: "What would you give a man who allows himself to be buggered?"

> "Oh, thirty shillings or two pounds, whatever you happen to have on you."

★ ★ ★

Criminal practice, of course, gives the opportunity for the blackest humour of all. Thus it is said that an item which actually did figure in a solicitor's bill of costs read:

"To attending your execution for murder when you were hanged."

A variant of this is the legendary item in an Irish bill of costs, quoted by the great James Comyn (see page 7):

"To attending you for the purposes of drawing your last will and testament but, on arrival, finding that you had already died, Five Guineas."

Yes, your honour, the statement was contemporaneous – that is why it is written in blood

Can it really be the case that, as one experienced circuit judge recounts, one client, having been cautioned, solemnly replied:

> "My solicitor has advised me that if I am innocent then I should tell my story, but if I am guilty I should say nowt… so I'm saying nowt"?

According to one writer,

> "A colleague was representing a young man whose mother was most concerned about the progress of his case. He explained tactfully that the son's interview, filled as it was with frightful lies and worse admissions, was rather a problem. 'I know,' she said, heartfelt and full of maternal concern. 'It's terrible – and I always brought up all my kids to go "no comment".'

Now, the "no comment" interview can get tedious, and in one police station the police officers and certain local solicitors whom they knew well were in the habit of enlivening proceedings by playing 'The Duck Game'. References to ducks (and waterfowl in general) had to be introduced into the record of interview. Thus:

> "This car, was it a shade of *duck-egg blue*?"

> "*Widgeon* do you mean?"

"I'm *grebed* that you *coot* pretend not to know."

"I am advising my client to exercise his right of silence, and to remain *mute*."

"Your client is *ducking* and diving."

After the inevitable happened and a transcript was read out in the Crown Court, one of the main culprits among the local lawyers was invited to step into the local cop-shop for a wigging from the Superintendent, whom he knew well:

"Mr ------, you have been getting my officers into trouble and this really has to stop."

"I *can 'ard*ly believe you said that. One point!"

Somehow, the solicitor concerned made it out of the police station in one piece.

As did a Circuit Judge who had spent the day at a meeting of Scout Commissioners and was somewhat hesitantly finding his way home through the pouring rain in an unfamiliar part of the country. Two bored cops decided that they would rather be in the police station than out on patrol, and pulled him over.

"Blow into this, sir..."

Although nothing stronger than Nescafé had passed his lips for a considerable time, His

Honour knew the rules and did as he was told.

"This is positive, sir. You are under arrest…"

Containing his surprise, His Honour allowed himself to be transported to the police station where, after being relieved of his belt and shoelaces lest he attempt to top himself, he was booked in.

"Name?"

"Occupation?"

At which point the Custody Sergeant vaguely started to wish he was somewhere else.

Now, you will be aware that the legal limit of alcohol in breath (unless you are reading this book in Scotland where they actually take road safety seriously) is 35 micrograms per 100 millilitres of breath. What you may not know is that there is a normal "background" figure of 5 micrograms, arising from normal metabolism.

Anyway, His Honour blew into the Alcotest machine. And produced a reading of 3 micrograms.

"Well, thank you, Sir, I think that clears that up…" said the Custody Sergeant.
"Not so fast" came the retort. *"I am entitled to the lower of two readings"*.

So the judge duly blew into the machine a second time. And came up with a reading of 2.

What the Custody Sergeant said to the two rain-averse constables as soon as the judge, wearing his belt and laces and an extremely broad grin, was out of earshot is unfortunately not recorded.

In court, rather than at the station, apparently the following exchange actually did take place:

Prisoner: As God is my judge, I am innocent!

Mr Justice Birkett (demonstrating the way with words which had made him the most feared and sought after advocate in the business): He isn't. I am. You're not.

Which was borrowed and adapted by Melford Stevenson (whom we met at page 16) in the line which regularly featured in his after-dinner speeches:

"Reggie Kray said only two true things at his trial. One, when he said prosecuting counsel was a fat slob. Two, when he said I was biased. He is. I was."

Birkett would have been proud of the response of a judge to a plea in mitigation offered on behalf of a client who had just been convicted of violent disorder:

"My Lord, you should know that my client comes from a broken home."

"From what I have just heard, I must suppose that he broke it himself."

★ ★ ★

It has been asserted that it really did occur that a hearing took place in Preston, and counsel found that a crucial document about which he needed to question a witness had been left in London:

Opposing counsel helpfully suggests, in a stage whisper: "Fax it up!"

Judge less helpfully observes: "Yes, it does, doesn't it?"

Back in London, of course, wigs and waistcoats are hot and uncomfortable during the summer months, and counsel inquired of the court usher about the air conditioning:

"It's controlled by the knob on the Bench."

came the informative reply. Counsel might have been better advised not to announce to the Judge
"I understand from the usher that your Lordship is in charge of the air-conditioning in the court."

★ ★ ★

In the dear departed days when criminal legal aid really existed, some IT genius computerised the forms. What happened next was wryly described by one District Judge (Magistrates Courts), as stipendiary magistrates or "Stipes" were snappily rebranded a few years ago:

> "The grant of a representation order here comes as a standard computer-generated form ending with 'Legal aid is granted for' and then the offence(s) for which the representation order has been granted. Our computer is struggling with the new offences under the Sexual Offences Act 2003. One of our local solicitors showed me a form which states 'Legal aid is granted for sexual intercourse with a woman'. He predicts a rash of similar applications once word gets out."

The opportunities for humour do not stop when the verdict is returned. Thus:

> "...one lifer at HM Prison Long Lartin sued the Home Office for the £1000 value of the holiday he might have won if some screw had not (allegedly) nicked the coupon from his Sunday Mail."

And I was informed by one colleague that

> "I had a case a couple of years ago where a

prisoner was suing the Home Office for not clearing his vacant cell quickly enough, thus enabling fellow cons to nick his stuff. He was outraged that everyone else's cell had not been searched.

His cell was vacant because he had done a runner".

You may not be too surprised to learn that that prisoner lost his case.

JURORS AND OTHERS

At the end of a criminal trial, the judge has to sum up the case to the jury. This brings its own problems.

The story is told of a trial being conducted in Beaumaris long before the days of the Welsh Language Act. The defendant was, as the technical term is, obviously as guilty as hell. Defence counsel asked the judge if, as an indulgence, he might make his closing speech in Welsh. The judge, being a fair-minded fellow and reckoning that this was the only indulgence the defence side was likely to get that day, agreed. Counsel addressed the jury briefly in Welsh, and sat down.

After a short retirement, the jury came back with an impeccably perverse verdict of Not Guilty.

On the way back to civilisation, defence counsel was asked what he had said to the jury. It translated approximately as:

"Members of the jury, prosecuting counsel is English; the judge is English. The defendant is Welsh. You are Welsh. Do your duty."

You might dismiss that tale as being apocryphal, but the Welsh language certainly secured one undeserved acquittal in the rather less Welsh-speaking south of the country.

Swansea council, reasonably enough, wished to stop HGVs from using a narrow road near an Asda store. So they put up a road sign reading NO ENTRY FOR HEAVY GOODS VEHICLES. RESIDENTIAL SITE ONLY. The Highways Department appreciated that the wording on the sign needed to be displayed both in English and in Welsh, but didn't have a Welsh speaker among their number, so emailed a request for it to be translated into Welsh.

They received the response, and duly added to their sign:

"NID WYF YN Y SWYDDFA AR HYN O BRYD. ANFONWCH UNRHYW WAITH I'W GYFIEITHU."

It was only when they attempted a while later to prosecute a driver who, though inconsiderate, was also both observant and Welsh-speaking that they discovered that they had actually sent the translation request at a time when the translator was on holiday and had set an automated message from his email account. A road sign which proclaims I'M NOT IN THE OFFICE AT THE MOMENT. SEND ANY WORK TO BE TRANSLATED. doesn't, apparently, satisfy the relevant Act of Parliament.

As Lord Denning once observed of some students who demonstrated in support of the Welsh language:

"They wish to do all they can to preserve the Welsh language. Well may they be proud of it. It is the language of the bards – of the poets and the singers – more melodious by far than our rough English tongue."

Not only the bards, poets and singers, you may think.

And speaking of Lord Denning – as in Anglesey, so in Sussex. Lord Denning ruefully recalled, from his time as a Law Lord, when he was sitting as chairman of Quarter Sessions during the vacation, as the rules then allowed:

"The first case I had at Lewes was a man who was charged with driving a car under the influence of drink. I summed up in my most impartial and impeccable manner. The jury came, I won't say to the most just result, they came to the usual result – they found him 'Not Guilty'.

So the next case I thought I'd try different tactics. This was a man who was charged with being in possession of house-breaking implements by night. This time I turned to the jury. I put on my most sarcastic and ironic manner. I said to them:

'Members of the jury, if you think the accused was at the door at midnight intending to present these implements to the householder as a gift –

as a tribute of esteem in which he held him –
then of course you will find him not guilty.'

They did."

To similar effect, a solicitor made an application for bail
on behalf of a man arrested for "going equipped".

He had not been intending to commit burglary,
explained the solicitor. He had been intending
to mend his bicycle.

With a bolt cutter, a hammer and a screwdriver.

Lord Denning, however, did not have to cope with the
jury who tried one Stephen Young for murder. They
took their time considering the verdict, and retired to a
hotel for the night. As recounted by Lord Chief Justice
Taylor:

"After dinner, there was conversation amongst
some of the jurors about ouija boards. One of
the bailiffs spoke out strongly against them, as
did a lady juror, and the other bailiff agreed,
telling them not to be so stupid. At about 11
p.m. the bailiffs conducted the jurors to their
rooms. Thereafter it is clear that four jurors, the
foreman and three women got together in the
room of one of the women. An ouija board was
set up…

At least some of those present began this procedure as a joke or 'harmless prank'. After purporting to receive messages from persons known or related to two of the jurors (one of them being deceased), the matter proceeded as follows, according to one of those present:

'Ray then asked, "Is anyone there?" The glass went to "yes". Ray said, "Who is it?" The glass spelt out "Harry Fuller". When I say the glass spelt it out, I mean it went to each letter. I realised Fuller was the subject of the evidence we were hearing. Ray said, "Who killed you?" The glass spelt out "Stephen Young done it".'

Unsurprisingly, the Court of Appeal allowed the appeal. But Mr Young's relief was short lived. He was convicted on a retrial and sentenced to life imprisonment.

A less extreme form of fortune telling was invoked by the late Judge Robert Lymbery, who in one of his first cases had to sentence a self-styled white witch, who had stolen an altar cross and candlesticks from a church. Lymbery gave the woman a suspended prison sentence but advised her to look into her crystal ball to see what would happen if she broke the law again.

"In case it is cloudy," he said, "I will tell you. You will go to prison."

Occasionally the jury, even without the assistance of an ouija board, can leave the judge wondering why he got out of bed that morning. In a trial for *handling stolen goods* at Snaresbrook Crown Court, the judge received a note from the jury saying:

> "We are satisfied that the defendant didn't steal the goods, and was only looking after them. We don't see the problem."

On another occasion, a defendant was being tried for possession of a kilo of top quality skunk (the issue being whether he was possessing with intent to supply or for personal use). Exhibit A was passed round the jury box. One deeply respectable female jury member clasped Exhibit A to her face and inhaled deeply... And the trial had to be adjourned until lunchtime for her to remember where her brain was supposed to be.

Some time later, the jury were about to retire. One bold jury member passed a note to the judge asking, "Could we take Exhibit A into the jury room?" The reply was terse, negative, and verged on the unparliamentary.

JUDGES...

I once made an impromptu speech at the launch of a Collaborative Law project, praising the idea. I do believe that collaboration can be a much better way of resolving some family disputes than going to court, and said as much: "I feel a bit like a turkey speaking up for Christmas – 'Stay Away From Court, Says Judge!'" Unfortunately, the choice of words came back to bite me when some extracts were used for publicity purposes and I was reported as saying:

"I feel like a bit of a turkey, says Judge."

Unsurprisingly, judges at all levels try to discourage people from rushing into litigation. It is as true now as when Lord Justice Russell made the comment in 1969 that

"Litigation is an activity that does not markedly contribute to the happiness of mankind."

Or as Mrs Justice Hogg put it in 2014, in a family case where litigation had rumbled on for over eight years, beginning when the child concerned was aged only three:

"Litigation is not conducive to peaceful existence. Litigation is anxiety-making. Litigation is aggravation to the lay parties. It does not help a peaceful life."

Lord Justice Ward in 2012 wisely observed:

"Not all neighbours are from hell. They may simply occupy the land of bigotry. There may be no escape from hell but the boundaries of bigotry can with tact be changed by the cutting edge of reasonableness skilfully applied by a trained mediator. Give and take is often better than all or nothing."

In another case in 2007 he had gone into specifics:

"The first extraordinary aspect of this bitterly-fought litigation is that the claimant has spent some £60,000 on it to date, the defendants £25,000; £85,000 in all, over a claim worth at most £23,500. Now, litigation must be fun if the parties are prepared to spend that much on a rollercoaster ride to judgment without pausing, either of them, to suggest that mediation would be a more sensible way to resolve their differences."

The couple before Lord Justice Ward were far from the only pair of litigants to generate extremely expensive red mist. Thus Mr Justice Holman in 2014, before

launching into a celebrated denunciation of the lawyers'
combined attack on the rain forests (see page 126):

> "What are they arguing about? They are arguing
> about a claimed half share in an asset that may
> be worth around £1 million. So they are arguing
> about £500,000. What they have incurred in
> costs is not far short of three times the amount
> in dispute. Others might use other words
> of description, but as this is a judgment in a
> courtroom, I will merely say that the costs, and
> also the scale and intensity of this litigation, have
> been, and are, completely disproportionate."

You cannot blame Ward for having started his judgment
with the observation that

> "This litigation fills me with despair."

That despair was shared by Lord Justice Millett in
1996. Ms Julie Burchill had expressed herself in
characteristic fashion concerning film director Steven
Berkoff. Having on an earlier occasion written:

> "... film directors, from Hitchcock to Berkoff,
> are notoriously hideous-looking people.",

she returned to the subject in a review of the film
'Frankenstein'. Describing a character in the film called
'the Creature', she wrote:

"The Creature is… rejected in disgust when it comes out scarred and primeval. It's a very new look for the Creature – no bolts in the neck or flat-top hairdo – and I think it works; it's a lot like Stephen Berkoff , only marginally better-looking."

Berkoff sued for libel. A majority of the Court of Appeal held that this nonsense should be put before a jury. Dissenting, Millett commented:

"I have no doubt that the words complained of were intended to ridicule Mr. Berkoff, but I do not think that they made him look ridiculous or lowered his reputation in the eyes of ordinary people. There are only two cases which have been cited to us which are at all comparable. In *Winyard v. Tatler Publishing Co.* (C.A. unreported: 16th June 1991) it was held to be defamatory to call a professional beautician 'an ugly harridan', not because it reflected on her professional ability, but because some of her customers might not wish to be attended by an ugly beautician. I find the decision difficult to understand…

The other case is *Zbyszko v. New York American Inc.* (1930) 2239 NYS 411. A newspaper published a photograph of a particularly repulsive gorilla. Next to it appeared a photograph of the plaintiff above the caption: 'Stanislaus Zbyszko, the Wrestler: Not Fundamentally Different from the Gorilla in Physique'. The Statement of Claim alleged that this had caused the plaintiff to be shunned and avoided by his wife (who presumably had not noticed her husband's physique until it was pointed out to her by the newspaper) his relatives, neighbours, friends and business associates, and had injured him in his professional calling. The New York Court of Appeals held that the caption was capable of being defamatory. The case was presumably cited to us as persuasive authority. I find it singularly unpersuasive except as a demonstration of the lengths of absurdity to which an enthusiastic New York lawyer will go in pleading his case.

...Miss Burchill made a cheap joke at Mr. Berkoff's expense; she may thereby have demeaned herself, but I do not believe that she defamed Mr. Berkoff.

If I have appeared to treat Mr. Berkoff's claim with unjudicial levity it is because I find it impossible to take it seriously. Despite the views of my brethren, who are both far more experienced than I am, I remain of the opinion that the proceedings are as frivolous as Miss Burchill's article. The time of the Court ought not to be taken up with either of them."

Unjudicial levity, perhaps, was displayed by Lord Justice

Ward (again) when he mischievously commenced a judgment with:

> "There I was, like the concierge of the Ritz hotel, which as we all know is always open. I was hiding away behind urgent bundles of authorities trying to write a reserved judgment when an application for a stay of execution landed on my desk at 6.50 pm on Friday."

Again, when deciding whether a businessman who had borrowed too much from several banks should have permission to appeal, he remarked:

> "The claimant accordingly engaged management consultants to stave off – and here I must warn myself not to fall into the error of Dr Spooner's ways – to stave off the warring bankers."

Lord Justice Otton nearly fell off his chair, mused Ward on one occasion, before going on to observe that the remark was well received in academic circles, save for the shining wits of All Souls'.

He would probably have approved of the suggestion which I have read that the collective noun for bankers should be a wunch.

Judicial levity most certainly was displayed by Mr Justice Melford Stevenson when he observed that

> "...living in Manchester is a wholly incomprehensible choice for any free man to make"

to say nothing of Lord Justice Lawton's suggestion on another occasion that

> "Wife beating may be socially acceptable in Sheffield but it is a different matter in Cheltenham."

The contrary vice of false modesty was avoided by Lord Justice Russell in *Thorne RDC v Bunting (No 2)* [1972]:

> "I am afraid I have dealt rather briefly with the extensive arguments that were put before us... because, in *my perhaps not very humble opinion*, there is absolutely nothing in the case and nothing in the appeal."

Russell was no match, however, for the Master of the Rolls of the Victorian era, Sir George Jessel. Jessel was probably one of the ablest judges this country has ever seen, and certainly one of the most self-confident. He was apparently asked by one of his colleagues, Lord Justice James, whether he had actually said "I may sometimes be wrong, but I never have any doubts". Jessel's reply was:

> "Very likely, but I did not say 'I may sometimes be wrong'."

* * *

'Hmm... "he cannot understand and retain relevant information" and "may make decisions that others think unwise". Well, that applies to most judges that I know'

One senior judge has rather rashly stated very publicly on more than one occasion that if anyone catches him using Latin in a judgment he will donate £100 to charity. Well, that is one way of ensuring that the Family Law Bar and the lawyers of Worcester College, Oxford, at any rate, read his judgments with close attention.

But using Latin has other hazards. I am indebted to a correspondent in the solicitors' trade paper, the *Law Society's Gazette*, for the information that

"The use of the expression 'per se' causes merriment in Finland. *Perse* is Finnish for 'arse'."

Who needs Latin, though, when you can manage the sort of elegant put-down which the late Mr Justice Hart managed? There is a procedure in civil litigation called an application for summary judgment, which allows one side to say, in effect, that the other side's case is such nonsense it shouldn't need a full trial to say so.

> "The court," states the relevant rule, "may give summary judgment against a claimant or defendant on the whole of a claim or on a particular issue if:
>
> (a) it considers that the claimant or defendant (as the case may be) has no real prospect of succeeding on the claim or issue; and
>
> (b) there is no other compelling reason why the case or issue should be disposed of at a trial."

Was that second paragraph a get-out?

> "A trial might provide opportunities for the display of forensic skill, might enable a wider public to interest itself in the salacious details of a relationship which both parties appear to have regretted, and would offer ample opportunities for lawyers' profit costs. None of these is an 'other compelling reason' for allowing this action to proceed to trial within the terms of Civil Procedure Rules Part 24."

Thud!

But Hart was left panting by the side of Mr Justice Rimer in *Chester City Council v Arriva Plc* (2007):

> "The claimants' policy appears to have been to ensure that they did not call a witness who knew anything about the relevant facts: far better instead to call one who knew nothing about them. It is a novel way to try to prove a case, but it is not one to be recommended."

One senior county court judge tells of

> a litigant who stormed out of his court actually smashing a plate glass door en route, and then stormed back into the court a few minutes later because he had forgotten that he was supposed to be disabled and had left his wheelchair in court.

To similar effect is the story of a judge very calmly trying crime, who was faced with a defendant who insisted that his (imaginary) dog must accompany him into the witness box. Everyone else, particularly prosecuting counsel, got terribly worked up about this but His Honour sat calmly as the defendant went into the witness box, tied up the (imaginary) lead and ordered Meta-Fido to sit.

The defendant gave his evidence. He was cross examined at some length, at the end of which he returned to the dock.

The judge leaned over.

"Mr ------," he said. "You've forgotten your dog."

The judge may not just have to deal with the parties. In *F.G. Hemisphere Associates LLC v. The Republic of Congo* (2005), Mr Justice Cooke had to deal with a case in which a 'vulture fund' (a fund which buys up 'distressed debt', especially distressed sovereign debt, at a knockdown price and then seeks to recover the face value of the debt from the debtor) was pursuing the Republic of Congo. The particular problem in the case was which of two vulture funds should have first call on some assets which had been recovered. Given the not very palatable subject matter, he can hardly be blamed for enlivening the report a little:

> "As the parties put forward their arguments, the court was subjected to a barrage of noise from a protest taking place outside the building, including music blaring from loudspeakers. Two of the more readily recognisable ditties were those of the themes from the films *The Great Escape* and *The Dambusters*. I decline to allow FGH to escape from the effect of their dilatoriness in pursuing this asset at any time before this, notwithstanding the well-publicised litigation which was taking place and initiated by Kensington. I further decline to bust the dam or open the flood-gates to allow all creditors of the Congo to latch onto this debt as a matter

of equitable discretion and to take advantage of
the fruits of Kensington's diligence".

And as well as the litigants, and the advocates, and the
demonstrators outside the court building, the Judge
has to cope with the jury.

The democratic glory of the jury system is, of
course, the power of the jury to bring in the verdict they
think right, irrespective of what the judge may think.
Generally, judges accept this as an occupational hazard,
but not always. Thus when, long ago, the future Lord
Denning, then A. T. Denning KC, persuaded a jury to
bring in a manslaughter verdict against his client who
Mr Justice Charles felt was plainly guilty of murder,
His Lordship bellowed:

"Get out of there. You have been untrue to your
oaths. You are not fit to be on a jury."

More recently, when a plausible defendant, accused of
sexual offences against children, impressed the jury far
more than the judge, some of the gloss may have been
taken off the verdict of 'not guilty' by the icy remark:

"Congratulations, members of the jury. You
have just allowed yourselves to be successfully
groomed by the defendant."

Whereupon the judge turned on his heel and stalked
out of the court.

**Your statement of case tells a story – and it's
a fairy story**

Sometimes in the course of a successful appeal the judge who is being appealed against comes in for the same treatment. Thus Judge Hurst at Aylesbury received the devastating assessment from Lord Justice Scott in 1942:

> "The county court judge, as Lord Greene MR has pointed out, has been in error in a great many of the sentences contained in his judgment on questions of law; indeed, there is hardly a sentence expressing a legal opinion in the judgment with which I do not disagree."

On one occasion, counsel even saved the Court of Appeal the trouble. I have not located the case in which it occurred, but according to no less an authority than Lord Neuberger, counsel once opened an appeal back in the late 19th century with:

> "My Lords, this is an appeal from Mr Justice Kekewich. However, there are other grounds of appeal…"

What is certainly the case is that when the *Solicitors' Journal* reported Kekewich's appointment to the Bench an anonymous correspondent felt moved to add:

> "We make the above announcement with a regret which we feel sure will be shared by the profession."

And of course it is possible for one member of the court to take a swipe at the other judges. During the early part of World War II, the Government invoked a notorious provision called Defence Regulation 18B, which permitted internment without trial. The Regulation actually said that someone could be interned if the Home Secretary *had reasonable cause* to suspect him of enemy sympathies. Some time in 1940, someone in the Home Office decided that it would be an awful lot more convenient if the requirement were just that the Home Secretary *thought that he had reasonable cause...*

Mr Justice Tucker at first instance and three judges in the Court of Appeal duly went along with this, as did four Law Lords, in what has cynically been described as "the Law Lords' contribution to the war effort". But Lord Atkin concluded a monumental dissenting speech with the withering (and, many have felt, entirely justified) observation:

"I know of only one authority which might justify the suggested method of construction. 'When I use a word,' Humpty Dumpty said in rather a scornful tone, 'it means just what I choose it to mean, neither more nor less.' 'The question is,' said Alice, 'whether you can make words mean different things.' 'The question is,' said Humpty Dumpty, 'which is to be master— that's all.' (Looking Glass, c. vi.) After all this long discussion the question is whether the words 'If a man has' can mean 'If a man thinks he has.' I am of opinion that they cannot, and that the case should be decided accordingly."

The whole of Atkin's speech is worth reading. Before concluding with a couple of pages of rhetoric – which included the unflattering assessment of the Government's lawyers

> "In this case I have listened to arguments which might have been addressed acceptably to the Court of Kings Bench in the time of Charles I"

– Atkin meticulously dissected the relevant regulation in a piece of legal analysis which is a model of its kind.

Often overlooked in the devastating rhetoric with which Atkin ended his speech is a subtle and cultured piece of praise for the laws of the United Kingdom.

> "In this country, amid the clash of arms,
> the laws are not silent. They may be changed, but
> they speak the same language in war as in peace."

Before going into the law, Atkin was an Oxford classical scholar, and familiar with the line from Cicero's oration *Pro Milone*: "*Silent enim leges inter arma*", commonly rendered as

> "Amid the clash of arms the laws are silent."

That "not", inconspicuously tucked away, is in some ways as moving as anything else Atkin said.

Nearly forty years later, in 1979, Lord Diplock, another great judge, though with a very different political outlook from Atkin's, had the grace to observe:

"For my part I think the time has come to acknowledge openly that the majority of this House in *Liversidge v. Anderson* were expediently and, at that time, perhaps, excusably, wrong and the dissenting speech of Lord Atkin was right."

There was a distinct echo of Atkin in 2004 when the House of Lords was invited, yet again, to uphold the Home Office's oft-desired power of interment without trial. The life of the nation was under threat from terrorism, their Lordships were told. Lord Hoffmann was having none of it:

"In my opinion, such a power in any form is not compatible with our constitution. The real threat to the life of the nation, in the sense of a people living in accordance with its traditional laws and political values, comes not from terrorism but from laws such as these. That is the true measure of what terrorism may achieve. It is for Parliament to decide whether to give the terrorists such a victory."

Lord Atkin was unimpressed by the courts under Charles I, but it was to the unjustly maligned James II that we owe an observation which was uncharacteristically modest for a member of the House of Stuart. Having dismissed all his judges and decided that he would judge all cases himself, James remarked:

> "There is nothing in it: this judging business is easy. I find I can make up my mind when I have heard the first party."

He had the honesty to add:

> "It is when I have heard both sides that things get difficult"

a difficulty which was acknowledged by Lord Ellenborough, an early-19th century Lord Chief Justice.

A friend who was a General was appointed Governor of a minor colony where he was also required to sit as a judge and was worried about that, as he had no legal experience.

> Lord Ellenborough told him not to worry as his common sense and vast experience in the Army making decisions based on who and what he believed would mean he would always get the right answer but that as he was not a lawyer he should never give his reasons because they would be always be wrong.

★ ★ ★

Sometimes the put-down is implicit. Long ago, one Magistrates' Court had a splendidly avuncular and helpful Clerk, and indeed most of his deputies were similarly helpful. But there was one Deputy Clerk to the Justices who was a notorious stickler for dotting every 'i' and crossing every 't' in sight.

There used to be a procedure in the Magistrates' Court called a "Section 9 Committal" where, in a serious case, the magistrates were presented with written statements and on the basis of them "committed" the defendant for trial at the Crown Court. This became a very routine process indeed in the hands of an experienced practitioner.

One day, the Clerk amiably expressed mild surprise at one prosecuting solicitor dealing with a committal in a rather pernickety fashion. The solicitor responded:

"Well, I suppose I might be being slightly over-careful. But if a certain clerk were sitting..."

"He's not here, is he? *Oh, yes, there he is,*"

beamed the Clerk, ostentatiously peering under his desk in full view of the Magistrates.

Occasionally, the put-down is affectionate. Thus, according to Lord Dyson, when they started televising the proceedings of the Supreme Court,

"I believe that the President of the Supreme Court, Lord Neuberger, commented that he had been told off by his wife and daughter for slouching on camera and having an evidently smug smile."

Neuberger, again, once observed that, reading a long and tedious judgment, he found himself 'losing the will to live'. This was, he admitted,

> "...particularly disturbing as I realised that it was one of my own judgments."

And sometimes the put-down doesn't even need to be there at all. When, after a string of successful appeals from his judgments, the Court of Appeal *upheld* a judgment of the then Mr Justice Henry, he is said to have remarked dryly:

> "Hmm. I still say I was right."

★ ★ ★

Judges, of course, come in several flavours. There are District Judges at the bottom of the food chain, with Circuit Judges, High Court Judges, the Court of Appeal and what is now the Supreme Court (whose members tend to be disrespectfully referred to as "the Supremes"), formerly the House of Lords, lording it (so to speak) over all they survey. And their respective roles have never been so well summed up as by a former District Judge:

> "I have always proceeded on the basis that the law will provide a remedy if the ordinary intelligent man would expect one. Lord Justice Mustill (as he then was) so advised Registrars

(as we then were) in the late 1980s. But he did go on to say that, if we were wrong, the Circuit Judge would put it right. He then went on to say that the Court of Appeal would naturally then restore the Registrar's decision. And that the House of Lords would then make a bog of it and confuse the whole issue. It was very shortly after this that he was ennobled."

Or, as the then Attorney General observed in 1950:

"The county court is a most important court. It is the people's court in the best and the good sense of that word... It is a court presided over by shrewd and kindly men, who get to know the habits and the social circumstances of the areas within their jurisdiction; and who administer justice, not from great Olympian heights, but in close contact with the people with whose cases they are dealing."

A view with which I would, of course, agree.

Another view of the judicial hierarchy was proffered by the irrepressible Lord Justice Ward, dissenting in a 2010 case where he was sitting in the Court of Appeal alongside Lords Justices Longmore and Stanley Burnton. After explaining why he disagreed with his colleagues and would have followed (as he saw it) a decision of Stanley Burnton as a first instance judge:

"There is little point in expanding upon these reasons for I am outnumbered, nay outgunned, by the commercial colossi seated either side of me. I prefer the instincts of the youthful Mr Justice Stanley Burnton before he became corrupted by the arid atmosphere of this Court. It goes to prove what every good old-fashioned county court judge knows: the higher you go, the less the essential oxygen of common sense is available to you. So I am unrepentant. With, of course, great respect to my Lords, I dissent."

Ah, yes, "with great respect". See the discussion of this expression under "Lawyers Speak in Code". I am also indebted to Sir Alan Ward for two views of the Court of Appeal, or indeed of appellate courts in general:

"The relationship of the appellate court to the judge being appealed against is similar to that of dog and lamp-post"

and the view that apparently originated with the Australians, that

"...the Court of Appeal are like soldiers who stay away from the battlefield and come down at night to shoot the wounded."

For sheer disrespectful mischief, however, nothing will ever match the retort of Sir James Hunt, who agreed to sit in the Court of Appeal only six weeks after undergoing surgery to remove a brain tumour:

> "Oh well, you only need half a brain to sit in the Court of Appeal."

...AND WOULD-BE JUDGES

The process of becoming a judge is, rightly, a difficult one. We no longer accept the idea of someone being made a High Court Judge as a reward for political services (which was the excuse for Edward Ridley – see page 16 – finding his way on to the Bench). The would-be judge has to complete a long application form and if successful in the "sift" faces a tough interview.

A few years ago there was understandable concern that appointees to the Bench *still* tended to be white, male, Public School educated, Oxbridge graduates, and so was born the inspired idea of making the "sift" solely on the basis of a blind-marked two hour written exam. This undoubtedly removed any unconscious bias in favour of white males, though one wonders which candidates were best equipped to face a two hour written exam. Where might they have gone to school, and from where might they have graduated?

Anyway, life imitated art. When I took the Judicial Appointments Commission's test a few years ago, several of us, recovering over a well-deserved black coffee afterwards, were reminded of Peter Cook's E. L. Wisty character who, having observed that he could have been a judge, but never had the Latin for the rigorous judging exams, explained that:

> "They're noted for their rigour. People come staggering out saying 'My God, what a rigorous exam'."

They were. We did.

Once you survive that, the interview faces you. I believe things may have changed, but there used to be a question: "Is there anything in your personal or private life which might be a source of embarrassment to the Lord Chancellor were it to become known?". The best answer ever given to that is thought to have been the response of one candidate who is said to have pursed his lips and said carefully,

> "Well, it *all* depends how *easily* the Lord Chancellor is embarrassed!"

★ ★ ★

Another question in the interview asks the candidate whether there is anything in their career which they really regret. A brilliant answer was given by one candidate who thought for a few moments and then said, with a completely straight face:

> "I was on the interviewing panel when a young member of the Bar was applying for a tenancy, and we turned her down. I did wonder whether

we had done the right thing, though it turned out all right in the end as I understand she secured a tenancy in another set of chambers. Because *I do think that it's the responsibility of the interviewing panel to help the candidate to give of their best – I'm sure you will agree."*

Deservedly, that candidate got appointed.

Occasionally, of course, appointments may be, shall we say, surprising. Though few advocates will be as forthright on the subject as the one and only F. E. Smith, at the end of a long and heated argument in the county court with His Honour Judge Willis. Demanded Willis: "What do you suppose I am on the Bench for, Mr Smith." With immaculately feigned courtesy, Smith responded:

> "It is not for me, your Honour, to attempt to fathom the inscrutable workings of Providence."

'Isn't it a relief that an unusual, eccentric or even bizarre lifestyle is no longer a conclusive test of capacity?'

LIONS

After Lord Atkin delivered his excoriating dissenting judgment in Liversidge's case, he received a letter from one of the judges of the High Court, the magnificently named Wintringham Stable. Stable commented:

> "I venture to think the decision of the House of Lords has reduced the stature of the judiciary, with consequences that the nation will one day bitterly regret. Bacon, I think, said the judges were the Lions under the throne, but the House of Lords has reduced us to mice squeaking under a chair in the Home Office."

Atkin, of course, was clear about the lion's duty to roar:

> "I view with apprehension the attitude of judges who on a mere question of construction when face to face with claims involving the liberty of the subject show themselves more executive minded than the executive. Their function is to give words their natural meaning, not, perhaps, in war time leaning towards liberty,

but following [what had been said by one of the other Law Lords in another case]: 'In a case in which the liberty of the subject is concerned, we cannot go beyond the natural construction of the statute.'... It has always been one of the pillars of freedom, one of the principles of liberty for which on recent authority we are now fighting, that the judges are no respecters of persons and stand between the subject and any attempted encroachments on his liberty by the executive, alert to see that any coercive action is justified in law...

I protest, even if I do it alone, against a strained construction put on words with the effect of giving an uncontrolled power of imprisonment to the minister."

He had, perhaps, learned from a good teacher. When a young barrister has passed the necessary exams and been "called to the bar", he or she must spend a period as a "pupil" in the company of an experienced barrister, known as a pupil master. Sometimes, the relationship is strained. I remember remarking of Judge ------ that even though he was a difficult tribunal he was a good lawyer.

"Oh, do you think so?" commented a member of the Bar who was present. *"He certainly wasn't when he was my pupil master."*

But to return to Atkin.

His pupil master had been Thomas Scrutton, who went on to be a member of what is generally thought to have been the strongest Court of Appeal the country has ever seen, curiously with his former pupil Atkin sitting alongside him.

Scrutton was a brilliant lawyer but tended at first to be a bit impatient with the *lawyers* appearing in front of him – though when Scrutton died, his obituary writer commented that "no *poor litigant appearing to plead his own cause in person* ever failed to find in Scrutton a genial, patient and helpful judge."

In fact, so rude was Scrutton to the lawyers, the leading London commercial solicitors clubbed together to brief counsel to appear before Scrutton in open court to ask him to be less abrasive, a request which apparently Scrutton took to heart.

In 1923, the Great War had ended but the guerrilla war for Irish independence had followed. One Art O'Brien, said to be a ringleader of the IRA, was living in London. At the request of the Government of the Irish Free State, he was summarily arrested and shipped to Dublin, though the term "extraordinary rendition" had not yet been invented. He sought habeas corpus. The Divisional Court refused. He appealed, and the appeal came before the celebrated court of Bankes, Scrutton and Atkin.

Scrutton did not mince his words:

"This appeal raises questions of great importance regarding the liberty of the subject, a matter on which English law is anxiously careful, and which English judges are keen to uphold. As Lord Herschell says... 'The law of this country has been very jealous of any infringement of personal liberty.' This care is not to be exercised less vigilantly, because the subject whose liberty is in question may not be particularly meritorious. It is indeed one test of belief in principles if you apply them to cases with which you have no sympathy at all. You really believe in freedom of speech, if you are willing to allow it to men whose opinions seem to you wrong and even dangerous; and the subject is entitled only to be deprived of his liberty by due process of law, although that due process if taken will probably send him to prison. A man undoubtedly guilty of murder must yet be released if due forms of law have not been followed in his conviction. It is quite possible, even probable, that the subject in this case is guilty of high treason; he is still entitled only to be deprived of his liberty by due process of law."

Scrutton went on to consider some of the Regulations which had been put into effect in Ireland and mused, unkindly,

"There appears to have been no careful consideration of which of these regulations were concerned with the restoration of order in Ireland, especially as far as this application to England was concerned, otherwise it is difficult to understand why in 1920 it was desirable for the restoration of order in Ireland to regulate the cultivation of hops in England (reg. 2 N N), or the keeping of pigs in England (reg. 2 N), or the capture for food of migrating birds or rabbits in England (reg. 2 R), or to limit English season tickets (reg. 7 B), or to forbid persons in England to have in their possession more silver coinage than they reasonably required (reg. 30 E E), or to provide for the discipline in England of the marine and military forces of His Majesty's Allies (reg. 45 F), and these are only a few of the regulations which are excellent for the defence of the realm in time of foreign war, but yet have nothing to do with the maintenance of law and order in Ireland. *Why these regulations were ever enacted in this lazy and unintelligent way I do not understand.*"

While the case was proceeding, the Government hastily introduced some new regulations. Scrutton was unimpressed:

"It is perhaps beyond the function of His Majesty's judges to criticise the advice which His Majesty's Ministers give to His Majesty as to the issuing of Orders in Council, but it may be permissible to say respectfully that it adds a new terror to litigation with Government officials if they can make Orders in Council while a case is being argued, to assist their argument."

"Grr!" indeed.

Oh, and in case you are supposing that all of this is just unworldly judges not appreciating things which the perceptive folk in the Home Office understand, eventually the Home Office revealed the reasons why they had interned Mr Liversidge, whose case provoked Atkin's wrath. They included:

"You are the son of a Jewish Rabbi."

In 1941. While Britain was at war with the Nazis. You couldn't make it up – but then, as Mark Twain said, quoted by Lord Justice Sedley, the difference between reality and fiction is that fiction has to be credible.

THE LUNCH ADJOURNMENT

A care case was proceeding in Manchester before an averagely grumpy High Court judge. One of the parties was represented by a fairly ancient silk, whose invariable practice was to put himself outside a three-course lunch every day. Each day the case was supposed to resume at two o'clock. Mr A---- QC made it back at 2.15, 2.20, 2.10... Eventually, on day four, he strolled into court at 2.30 pm. The Judge had had enough.

> "Mr A----, you have been late every day this week. What is your explanation?"

> "My Lord... Pudding!"

There is some truth in the saying that if you look the man in the eye and sound confident you will often get away with it. This proved to be the case.

As happened in another case in which the guardian ad litem and counsel for the child, both of them elegant ladies in their early fifties, returned late after lunch having very obviously just had their hair done.

They had calculated well. The judge before whom they were listed was male.

"You're very late"

"Well, your Honour, the queues in the sandwich shop were dreadful."

Which may, I suppose, have been true, although almost certainly irrelevant. At all events, His Honour merely harrumphed and proceeded with the case, to the astonishment of the other (female and observant) advocates spluttering in the front row.

I found myself looking the man in the eye when, as a very junior solicitor some 35 years ago, I was feeling conscientious and thought I ought to learn about the far-reaching changes to the welfare benefit system which were being introduced. The Child Poverty Action Group was organising a one-day seminar in London, which I resolved to attend; it was ten days into my summer holiday, but, as I say, I was young and conscientious in those days.

I remember three things about that seminar. One was that I was one of only two solicitors in private practice attending it, the other being the great (and now sadly deceased) Henry Hodge. Another was that I staggered out of the seminar a quarter of an hour before the end with a splitting headache and the feeling that I couldn't take any more. And...

Somewhat unusually, this seminar did not provide lunch. This was in the days before every third shop in central London was a sandwich bar, so I was faced with trying to find somewhere I could get lunch at reasonable cost and in a hurry. I accordingly breezed into the Law Society's Hall, lunched in the self-service cafeteria, and breezed out again.

I was appropriately attired for a CPAG welfare benefit seminar. I suspect that the appearance around the Law Society's Hall a few weeks after that visit of notices sternly observing that

MEMBERS ARE RESPECTFULLY REMINDED TO OBSERVE APPROPRIATE STANDARDS OF DRESS. FOR GENTLEMEN THIS WILL NORMALLY MEAN JACKET AND TIE...

just *may* have been connected with a young man in denim jacket and jeans and with ten days' growth of beard strolling confidently into the place.

AFTER THE CASE IS FINISHED...

Losing the case is bad enough. Losing the costs is worse. And the result of annoying the judge beyond endurance can be worse still. Thus Mr Justice Christopher Clarke in the Commercial Court in 2013, having endured a five month trial with a mind-boggling 373 trial bundles – the directions which allowed Mr Justice Holman to explode to such good effect do not apply in the Commercial Court – in a case which he described as

"...based on no sound foundation in fact or law"

and which had

"...met with a resounding, indeed catastrophic, defeat",

was forthright in his assessment of the men behind the claimant company:

"...Mr W---- was a man long on assertion and confidence, but short on analysis and understanding. He has pursued this litigation as if it was an act of war. He took positive salesmanship beyond the point of acceptability."

In an elegant dismissal of the claims, he observed:

"The claims put forward were an elaborate and artificial construct which, as [counsel for the defendant], in my view not inaccurately, puts it, were reverse engineered from the position in which the W----s found themselves on the facts. They were replete with defects, illogicalities and inherent improbabilities."

A withering assessment of one of the heads of claim was:

"The claim in deceit was such that Mr W----, the alleged victim, could not explain how he had been deceived."

And the conclusion was

"It has been said that a claimant is fortunate if he wins on every point. In this case the claimant has lost on every material issue. This was more than a misfortune. It arose because of the inherent defects in the claims in the light of the true facts."

You can understand the judge observing that

"I have been spared sight of much of the 5,000

pages of inter solicitor correspondence. It is apparent to me, however, from what I have seen that some of the correspondence from Clifford Chance has been voluminous and interminable, in some circumstances highly aggressive and in others unacceptable in content."

I was told long ago that the first rule of writing any letter was to imagine it being read out in a sarcastic tone of voice to a hostile judge. Quite so.

No surprises that the judge ordered the unsuccessful claimant to pay its opponent's costs on the more generous of the available bases of assessment.

It is also less than wise to rush into print while the judge is considering his judgment – as happened in 2014 with the first non-lawyer Lord Chancellor for several centuries, while the court was considering challenges to changes to the legal aid scheme. Lord Justice Alan Moses' withering comment could also appear under "Demob-Happy Judge" as it was his last judgment before retiring:

"Unrestrained by any courtesy to his opponents, or even by that customary caution to be expected while the court considers its judgment, and unmindful of the independent advocate's appreciation that it is usually more persuasive to attempt to kick the ball than your opponent's shins, the Lord Chancellor has reiterated the rationale behind [the changes]…"

ABOUT SOLICITORS

Now of course, having been one myself, I mustn't be too hard on solicitors. But occasionally others find it necessary to be.

Thus Lord Justice Rimer in a case in 2014:

"[The solicitor] imprudently chose to take the matter on and proceeded to discharge his retainer with an unusual lack of professionalism. His failure to make attendance notes is one example. In addition, he did not, certainly in 2007, give any clear advice… as to the nature and effect of the alterations covenant. He knew, at any rate down to 21 December 2007, that she was continuing the works; he had not told her to stop them; and his game plan, insofar as he had any, was apparently a hope that he could negotiate something with H&W, although he took no practical steps to do so. His handling of the case, in 2007, was a professional disgrace."

The trip to the Appeal Court proved worthwhile, however, because the damages awarded for the solicitor's negligence were drastically reduced. No such luck for the solicitor who found himself on the end of a tongue-lashing from the President of the Queen's Bench Division in a 2013 case:

> "...we reject as entirely dishonest his explanation that he has given us today. No person who is competent to act as a solicitor, let alone be the senior partner of a firm, let alone supervise others, and let alone to bring proceedings before this court *could possibly be as ignorant as he claims to be.*"

Though ignorance is not confined to solicitors. Lord Justice Salmon (who when he went to the House of Lords kept an imperturbably straight face when choosing to be known as Lord Salmon *of Sandwich*) was less than impressed with the directors of Dr Savundra's infamous insurance company, Fire Auto & Marine:

> "There were other directors, but it would appear that either they were exceptionally stupid or knew little more about the affairs of the company than its postal address."

But returning to solicitors, it has to be admitted that sometimes solicitors' time sheets claim improbable amounts of time. There is force behind the joke which has a solicitor encountering St Peter at the Pearly Gates:

St Peter: Before I let you in, can you just clarify something for me. How old were you when you died?

Solicitor (sadly): I was very young. I was only 47.

St Peter: That's funny. According to your timesheets you must have been at least 85.

And here's our specialist team that creates all the traps for solicitors to fall into

Spoiler alert. If you have not read *Strong Poison* by Dorothy L. Sayers and/or do not wish to know whodunit, turn to the next chapter now.

It is often difficult for lawyers to be liked. I remember as a young law student attending a meeting addressed by the one and only Lord Denning, when the great man beamed at his eager audience and began, in his distinctive Hampshire burr:

> "Let's get one thing straight. You're going to be unpopular. All lawyers are!"

A thought which has often comforted me over the years, I must say. To similar effect, I suppose, is the observation attributed to American Supreme Court Justice Sandra Day O'Connor:

> "There is no shortage of lawyers in Washington, DC. In fact, *there may be more lawyers than people.*"

And one High Court Judge, explaining why she went into the law, recalled:

> "I was in the debating team in the upper sixth at school, and went to debate at another school. We did well, and beat them. The teacher from the other side took it personally, and told me I should become a barrister, which was not meant as a compliment. I had a place at university to read English and I changed it to study Law."

But even if we have always been unpopular, there was a time when we were respected – as I was forcefully reminded once, while relaxing with a good book.

Many years ago, I had decided to re-read Dorothy L. Sayers' classic *Strong Poison* and borrowed a copy from Bedford library.

About halfway into the story (page 90 of the paperback) Lord Peter Wimsey is discussing the will of Mrs Wrayburn with Urquhart, the solicitor. While sententiously observing that his professional instinct is to avoid disclosing a client's affairs, Urquhart informs Wimsey that he is himself the beneficiary under the Wrayburn will..

A previous borrower had written, boldly and angrily, in the margin:

"RIDICULOUS! NO SOLICITOR WOULD EVER BEHAVE IN THIS WAY!"

It is only when, in the last few pages of the book, Wimsey establishes that *Urquhart had in fact poisoned his cousin with arsenic and contrived to frame Harriet Vane for the crime, being willing to see her hang for it*, that the deliciously ironic flattery of the marginal comment becomes clear.

THE DELIGHTS OF TELLING
PEOPLE TO GET LOST

There is a particular skill in telling someone to go away in the most memorable terms. Probably the most famous example of the kind arose in 1971, in what has been known forever after as *Arkell v. Pressdram* [unreported].

A solicitor who really should have known better at Messrs Goodman Derrick & Co. penned the following averagely pompous letter before action:

"We act for Mr Arkell who is Retail Credit Manager of Granada TV Rental Ltd. His attention has been drawn to an article appearing in the issue of *Private Eye* dated 9th April 1971 on page 4. The statements made about Mr Arkell are entirely untrue and clearly highly defamatory. We are therefore instructed to require from you immediately your proposals for dealing with the matter. Mr Arkell's first concern is that there should be a full retraction at the earliest possible date in *Private Eye* and he will also want his costs paid. His attitude to damages will be governed by the nature of your reply."

Unfortunately, those at the *Eye* reckoned they had done their homework properly, and the hapless solicitor received in reply:

> "We acknowledge your letter of 29th April referring to Mr J. Arkell. We note that Mr Arkell's attitude to damages will be governed by the nature of our reply and would therefore be grateful if you would inform us what his attitude to damages would be, were he to learn that the nature of our reply is as follows:
>
> Fuck off."

At which point, according to most accounts, the correspondence ended; but it seems that in fact Mr Arkell was so unwise as to issue proceedings. Eventually, Mr Arkell left Granada and decided to cut his losses, including paying the *Eye*'s costs.

The *Eye*'s comment was brutal and to the point:

> "Mr Arkell has now, albeit belatedly, complied with the suggestion made to him at an earlier stage of the proceedings."

And, of course, the luckless Mr Arkell has earned a particular sort of minor immortality.

Quite neat, and a clear refutation of the calumny

which states that Americans don't do irony, was the reply which was sent to a letter which one Dale O. Cox, Counsellor at Law, of Akron, Ohio, was so rash as to send to the Cleveland Browns in 1974:

> "Gentlemen,
>
> I am one of your season ticket holders who attends or tries to attend every game. It appears that one of the pastimes of several fans has become the sailing of paper airplanes generally made out of the game program. As you know, there is the risk of serious eye injury and perhaps an ear injury as a result of such airplanes. I am sure that this has been called to your attention and that several of your ushers and policemen witnessed the same.
>
> Please be advised that since you are in a position to control or terminate such action on the part of fans, I will hold you responsible for any injury sustained by any person in my party attending one of your sporting events. It is hoped that this disrespectful and possibly dangerous activity will be terminated."

What *did* get terminated, and with fairly extreme prejudice, was Mr Cox. He received a letter two days later which laconically said:

> "Dear Mr Cox,
>
> Attached is a letter that we received on

November 19, 1974. I feel that you should be aware that some asshole is signing your name to stupid letters.

Very truly yours,
James N. Bailey, General Counsel."

It is apparently proposed that the legal services' complaints procedure should extend to people who are not clients of the solicitors' firm concerned. One can, perhaps, have some sympathy with the anonymous solicitor writing to the *Law Gazette* who commented:

"One of my few remaining pleasures in practising is telling obnoxious, loudmouth, know-it-all non-clients to bugger off."

But the London solicitor who emailed his opponent with the request,

"Could you for once make an effort to behave like a normal person instead of a complete plonker?"

got disciplined for his efforts. He probably did not improve matters by writing of the opponent's two clients:

"We will give access to two people at our office to inspect the original documents. Mr Tweedledum can attend with his solicitor but not Mr Tweedledee."

"ONLY IN AMERICA..."

...as my grandmother used to murmur on occasion.

Stories of the goings on in the courts of the USA are legion, and some of them must surely be apocryphal – such as the delightful one which is familiar but bears repetition:

> During a trial in a small town, a witness was sworn in with her hand on the Bible – the standard admonitions to tell the truth, the whole truth and nothing but the truth, so help her God.
>
> The witness was a proper, well-dressed, elderly lady – the Grandmother type – well-spoken and poised.
>
> The prosecuting attorney approached the woman and asked, 'Mrs Jones, do you know me?' She responded, 'Why, yes I do know you, Mr Williams. I've known you since you were a young boy and frankly, you've been a big disappointment to me. You lie, cheat on your wife, manipulate people and talk badly about them behind their backs. You think you're a

rising big shot when you haven't the sense to realize you never will amount to anything more than a two-bit, paper-pushing shyster. Yes, I know you quite well.'

The lawyer was stunned. He couldn't even think for a few minutes. Then, slowly backed away, fearing the looks on the judge and jurors' faces, not to mention the court reporter who documented every word. Not knowing what else to do, he pointed across the room and asked, 'Mrs Jones, do you know the defense attorney?' She again replied, 'Why, yes, I do. I've known Mr Bradley since he was a youngster, too. He's lazy, bigoted, has a bad drinking problem. The man can't build or keep a normal relationship with anyone, and his law practice is one of the worst in the entire state. Not to mention he cheated on his wife with three different women. Yes, I know him.'

The defense attorney almost fainted and was seen slipping downward in his chair, looking at the floor. Laughter, mixed with gasps, thundered throughout the courtroom; the audience was on the verge of chaos.

The judge brought the courtroom to silence, called both advocates to the bench, and in a very quiet voice said, 'If either of you morons asks her if she knows me, you're going to jail.'

(See also "Never ask a question to which you don't know the answer" on page 130.)

Not apocryphal at all – I have seen a copy of the order in question – is the following. We all get annoyed with people from time to time, but can only dream of responding quite as spectacularly as United States District Judge Sam Sparks of Texas:

"ORDER Be it remembered on the 21st day of July 2004 and the Court took time to make its daily review of the above-captioned case, and thereafter, enters the following:

When the undersigned accepted the appointment from the President of the United States of the position now held, he was ready to face the daily practice of law in federal courts with presumably competent lawyers. No one warned the undersigned that in many instances his responsibility would be the same as a person who supervised kindergarten. Frankly, the undersigned would guess the lawyers in this case did not attend kindergarten as they never learned how to get along well with others. Notwithstanding the history of filings and antagonistic motions full of personal insults and requiring multiple discovery hearings, earning the disgust of this Court, the lawyers continue ad infinitum.

On July 20, 2004, the Court's schedule was interrupted by an emergency motion so the parties' deposition, which began on July 20, would and could proceed until 6:30 in the evening. No intelligent discussion of the issue was accomplished prior to the filing and service of the motion, even though the lawyers were in the same room. Over a telephone conference, the lawyers, of course, had inconsistent statements as to the support of their positions. On July 20, 2004, the Court entered an order allowing the plaintiffs/counter-defendants until July 23, 2004, two days from today, to answer a counterclaim. Yet, on July 21, 2004, Bodyworx.com, Inc.'s lawyers filed a motion for reconsideration of that Court order arguing the pleadings should have been filed by July 19, 2004.

The Court simply wants to scream to these lawyers, 'Get a life' or 'Do you have any other cases?' or 'When is the last time you registered for anger management classes?' Neither the world's problems nor this case will be determined by an answer to a counterclaim, which is four days late, even with the approval of the presiding judge. If the lawyers in this case do not change, immediately, their manner of practice and start conducting themselves as competent to practice in the federal court, the Court will contemplate and may enter an order requiring the parties to obtain new counsel.

In the event it is not clear from the above discussion, the Motion for Reconsideration is denied."

Judge Sparks returned to the fray in *Morris v Coker & Others,* 26 August 2011, with the following:

BE IT REMEMBERED on this day the Court reviewed the files in the above-styled causes, and now enters the following opinion and orders...

Greetings and Salutations!

You are invited to a kindergarten party on Thursday September 1, 2011, at 10.00 am in Courtroom 2 of the United States Courthouse, 200 W Eighth Street, Austin, Texas.

The party will feature many exciting and informative lessons, including:

How to telephone and communicate with a lawyer;

How to enter into reasonable agreements about deposition dates;

How to limit depositions to reasonable subject matter;

Why it is neither cute nor clever to attempt to quash a subpoena for technical failures of service when notice is reasonably given; and

An advanced seminar on not wasting the time of a busy federal judge and his staff because you are unable to practice law at the level of a first year law student.

Invitation to this exclusive event is not RSVP.
Please remember to bring a sack[3] lunch. The
United States Marshals have beds available if
necessary, so you may wish to bring a toothbrush
in case the party runs late."

This promptly inspired at least one of his colleagues
to try and go one better. Thus the letter sent to the
attorneys the following month by Judge Peggy Ableman
of Delaware:

"Dear Counsel,

In view of the recent correspondence regarding
the Anderson and Morgan trials, the Court has
decided that it is necessary to invite all counsel,
including pro hac vice attorneys, to appear
at the New Castle County Courthouse in
Wilmington, Delaware, on Sunday, September
4, 2011, for a 'special' emergency refresher
course in first year ethics and civility.
    While this may seem, at first blush, to be
merely an invitation for extracurricular credit,
this gathering is, in reality, mandatory, and
special arrangements have been made for entry
through the back door adjacent to the judges'
parking lot. Coffee and doughnuts will be
supplied for breakfast; lunch and dinner will
be ordered in at counsel's expense. Attendees

---

3   Yes, that's what the man wrote. He was contemplating drowning
counsel in a butt of their own Malmsey, presumably.

are encouraged to bring sleeping bags, toothbrushes, teddy bears, and jammies,[4] as the agenda will be exhaustive given the Court's assessment of the extraordinary need for this education.

The agenda will feature such fundamental and informative topics that have apparently been forgotten as a result of months of obsolescence[5], including but not limited to:

1. The importance of civility and professionalism when litigating in the Courts of Delaware;

2. The consequences of knowingly making misrepresentations in pleadings, filings and correspondence with the Court;

3. The expectations of Delaware Superior Court judges in connection with the preparation for and presentation of asbestos litigation;

4. Why it is not professional to whine or complain, either publicly or privately, about the amount of work that this Court requires or that asbestos litigation entails, particularly in light of

---

4   These terms reflect the Court's impression of the childish level to which this litigation has stooped.

5   This topic is of particular interest to the Court since counsel's inability to be civil and reasonable with one another does not typically occur in other civil cases involving only Delaware counsel.

the excessively large amount of fees generated by this litigation; and

5.   The reasons why this Court may, in this and future episodes of incivility, permit only Delaware counsel to participate at trial.

At the conclusion of this first year refresher course, the Court may proceed to discuss the issues that have been raised in the pretrial stipulation as well as any pending motions in limine.

While attendance is mandatory for all attorneys involved in these cases, there will be no grades reported nor will credit, extra or otherwise, be given. Extra credit to counsel will be considered only in the event that counsel are able to meet and confer prior to Sunday morning. In the event of settlement, the Court may reconsider scheduling this seminar to a later, more convenient date, or hold it on an "as needed" basis.

The Court is mindful that this invitation is on short notice and that it will have the effect of disrupting counsels' Labor Day holiday plans. Counsel should be advised, however, that the Court has also had plans for this weekend, as it has done for many of the weekends throughout the past sixteen months, and that the demands of this litigation on the Court are at least as rigorous, if not more so, as those that the Court has imposed upon the parties."

While both Judge Ableman and Judge Sparks got into some difficulties with their superiors (and Judge Ableman has, apparently, now left the Bench and gone back into private practice, where no doubt she astonishes everyone by her immaculate civility and professionalism), I suspect there will be a lot of judges on both sides of the pond murmuring, "I wish..."

AND BACK ON THIS SIDE
OF THE POND...

Few judges have been as capable as the late Lord
Denning of waxing lyrical in the course of a judgment,
but Denning surpassed himself in 1968 when the
trustees of a family settlement asked the court to
sanction a variation of the trusts of the settlement to
allow it to be moved to Jersey.

> "There are many things in life more worth-
> while than money. One of these things is to
> be brought up in this our England, which is
> still 'the envy of less happier lands'. I do not
> believe it is for the benefit of children to be
> uprooted from England and transported to
> another country simply to avoid tax... here the
> family had only been in Jersey three months
> when they presented this scheme to the court.
> The inference is irresistible: The underlying
> purpose was to go there in order to avoid tax. I
> do not think that this will be all to the good for
> the children. I should imagine that, even if they
> had stayed in this country, they would have had

a very considerable fortune at their disposal, even after paying tax. The only thing that Jersey can do for them is to give them an even greater fortune. Many a child has been ruined by being given too much. The avoidance of tax may be lawful, but it is not yet a virtue. The court of Chancery should not encourage or support—should not give its approval to it—if by so doing it would imperil the true welfare of the children, already born or yet to be born.

There is one thing more. I cannot help wondering how long these young people will stay in Jersey. It may be to their financial interest at present to make their home there permanently, but will they remain there once the capital gains are safely in hand, clear of tax? They may well change their minds and come back to enjoy their untaxed gains. Is such a prospect really for the benefit of the children? Are they to be wanderers over the face of the earth, moving from this country to that, according to where they can best avoid tax? I cannot believe that to be right. Children are like trees: they grow stronger with firm roots.

The long and short of it is, as the judge said, that the exodus of this family to Jersey is done to avoid English taxation. Having made great wealth here, they want to quit without paying the taxes and duties which are imposed on those who stay. So be it. If it really be for the benefit of the children, let it be done. Let them go, taking their money with them, but, if it be not truly for their benefit, the court should not countenance it. It should not give the scheme its blessing."

Children are like trees. Only Denning could have said it.

DEMOB-HAPPY JUDGE ALERT...

Occasionally a judge allows himself a little latitude at the end of his career. Thus Sir Alan Ward, having to his regret been obliged to hold that a houseboat owner was liable to pay council tax:

"...I am afraid, therefore, that Randy Northrop must lose and the appeal must be dismissed. I have a sneaking sympathy for him because he did not use many of the services which council tax is supposed to provide and it may have been harsh to list him in band A. But all of that is of no moment. He had indicated that he was soon to move and he has moved from the mooring. He has thrown off the bow lines and sailed away from the safe harbour though whether to catch the trade winds in his sails or just withstand the buffetings of the gales in the English Channel I know not. In as much as this is the penultimate judgment I shall write after 18 years in the Court of Appeal, I am a kindred spirit who has sailed away from the safe harbour of the Royal Courts of Justice, not at all

sure how to explore, or what to dream or what
I am about to discover."

★ ★ ★

And similarly, His Honour Judge Cowell. In August
2009, a Rolls Royce was involved in an accident. It was
one of a fleet of seven vehicles owned by a partnership.
That did not stop Accident Exchange Ltd claiming
£99,439.06, with a daily rate of about £2,000, for hire
successively of a Bentley and a Rolls Royce. We learn
of what Judge Cowell had to say from the judgment in
the Court of Appeal.

**I'm glad to say that the law is crystal clear Mr Bumper
– you can hire a reasonable car at a reasonable rate
for a reasonable time for reasonable repairs, and incur
reasonable delivery charges. But, naturally, what is
'reasonable' is not at all clear...**

He began his judgment by saying that it was "almost the last judgment I shall ever give after 15 years of doing justice according to law to the best of my ability". He went on:

> "1... This case raises the moral question which has occasioned me much anxious thought, whatever answer the law gives to the facts of this case which has occasioned further even more anxious thought, whether the ever increasing insurance premiums of the ordinary motorist, particularly one struggling to make ends meet and needing a modest car to go to work, should in some part be used so that the rich may continue at no expense to themselves to be filled with good things[6], that they think they need.
>
> 2... The claim was defended both as to liability and as to quantum. The temptation to give a perverted judgment on liability against the claimant in order to avoid all questions of quantum was very great, but conscience and my judicial oath meant that the temptation was successfully resisted."

At paragraph 3 of his judgment, he noted the appellant's evidence that he was in the property business dealing with millionaires and related investments and used

---

6   An elegantly barbed allusion to St Luke, chapter 1, verse 53.

the Rolls Royce "to maintain the correct impression in such circles". He needed "to maintain his image and that of his partnership . . . maintenance of an image of success was paramount". Cowell commented:

> "Well, what a testament that is to the superficial if not false nature of the warped values of society."

Just for good measure, he then quoted a verse from Hilaire Belloc's poem about the elephant who is supplied with many tons of hay a day.

This was apparently said by Mr Williams, counsel for the hire company, to amount to "facetious comment".

Surely not.

Tut-tutting with faces as straight as Their Lordships could manage, the Court of Appeal dismissed the appeal.

THE OLD ONES ARE STILL
THE BEST...

Ever since Shakespeare had Dick the Butcher say to Jack Cade in *Henry VI, Part 2* "The first thing we do, let's kill all the lawyers.", there has been a plentiful supply of a certain sort of lawyer-joke.

This one can stand for all:

A man takes his pet crocodile into a bar. He goes up to the barman and asks, "Do you serve lawyers?"

The barman, somewhat surprised, replies, "Of course, Sir. We serve anybody."

"Great!" says the man. "A pint of bitter for me and a lawyer for the crocodile."

Cheers.